Teach Yourself
SPANISH
Level Two

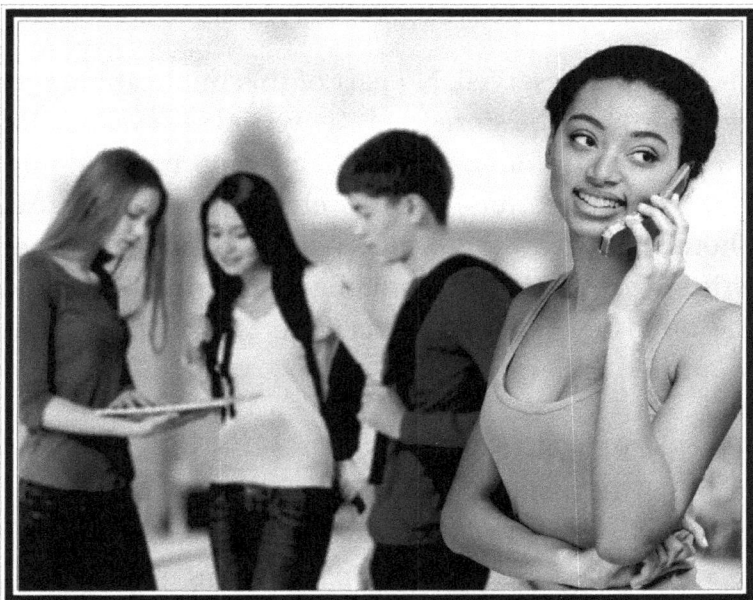

A complete Spanish course with Audio
Dr. Yeral E. Ogando

Teach Yourself Spanish - Level Two
© 2017 by Yeral E. Ogando
Publisher: Christian Translation LLC
Printed in the USA
Cover Design by SAL media

ISBN 13: 978-1-946249-05-0
ISBN 10: 1-946249-05-X

1. Language Learning 2. Spanish Language

DEDICATION:

This book is dedicated to the Unique and forever-lasting person who has always been there for me, no matter how stubborn I am:
GOD

I also want to dedicate this work to Sharon A. Lavy, who has given me the push I needed to write this book and to YOU (the reader), because you have taken the moment to read this incredible story and without you I would not have been here.

You all have a special place in my heart.

Always.

ACKNOWLEDGMENTS:

Gratitude to my Lord God for giving me the opportunity to write this book; Teach Yourself Spanish, dedicated to God above all, then to my daughters Yeiris & Tiffany, without them, this book would not be possible.

I also want to dedicate this work to all of you, who want to succeed in life and special to Gladys de Contreras, who has helped me through the process of getting the final edition and Franklin Guerra Castro for his talented voice in the audio.

This book has been inspired by all of you, thus providing you with an easy and comprehensive tool to learn the language quickly.

I encourage you to study the content of this book and you will see positive results in short time.

God bless you all

Dios les bendiga

Dr. Yeral E. Ogando

www.aprendeis.com

Table of Contents

Introduction

I have published this method for you to learn this language in a very quick and comprehensive way.

I kindly ask you to take 20 minutes of your time on a daily basis without interruption, so you can concentrate and digest the content of this work.

One of the biggest challenges in learning is to be a Self-Taught person, in other words, learn by yourself, it requires lots of discipline and dedication in your study. To study a full hour every day would make you feel tired and bored very quickly, that's why I recommend to you a minimum of 20 minutes per day and a maximum of 40 minutes per day, therefore, you will be achieving better results.

I wish you good luck in this amazing trip to the world of learning, and remember "Be shameless to speak."

Dr. Yeral Ogando
www.aprendeis.com

Before starting

Some people think and even say that you do not need to study the grammar of a language to learn it well. I humbly disagree with them. The non-grammar method could work with children, who have their minds ready for anything that you might feed them with; they have no worries, jobs, problems, so they are ready for it, but for adults with all our worries, responsibilities and most of the time, tired from work; it simply does not work. Our minds are already saturated with all kinds of stuff, so we need a way to really learn the language. After learning more than 10 languages, I have managed to master them and learn them very quickly because I have learned the pattern and short cuts for each language. I have also seen in my many years of teaching experience that you cannot learn a foreign language very well, if you don't know your own language. Thus, as you will see, you will learn your own language while studying a foreign language. This method is about recognizing and learning how to use the patterns on each grammar point.

I do not want you to learn words or phrases by heart, on the contrary, I want you to take your time and learn slowly by understanding each grammar point that I explain in this book. Your challenge is to recognize the patterns that I am teaching you. Once you recognize them and understand the structure of the language, you will improve your learning and speaking skills at a tremendous speed. Once again, pay close attention to the patterns, learn them, study them and then build your own Spanish world and vocabulary.

I am giving you the perfect tool to learn Spanish. You will be surprised to see how fast you can learn to recognize words. The texts in this book are up to date and modern Spanish for this generation, so be ready to improve your skills.

If you still have not downloaded your MP3 Audio files, check our BONUS PAGE for the DOWNLOAD.

I recommend that you always read aloud, so you can listen to yourself and compare the pronunciation with the one in the MP3 Audio. If you have any issues with the pronunciation, remember to check the **Pronunciation Chart**.

Teach Yourself Spanish is a powerful method that combines everyday conversation with real people, through grammar drills along with a vocabulary after every section. Pay close attention to the way people speak.

Grammar Explanations is a section that you need to make sure to understand and digest before moving to the next section. This book has been created to serve as a conversational and grammar at the same time. I have explained in details how to use the grammar in everyday conversation to help you master the language.

Do not forget that it is more effective to study a few minutes a day than to attempt to study a big portion occasionally. Your concentration will be best taken advantage of with 20 minutes of daily study.

Dr. Yeral E. Ogando

Steps on how to use this book for better results

Go to the *BONUS* page for the instructions on how to download the MP3 Audio files. That is your first step. Your best companion and tool "the *AUDIO* file".

Lesson 1 will teach you everything about the alphabet, reading and writing Spanish. Work on lesson one along with the Audio to master the sounds and pronunciation. Take notes of any new words or phrase that you do not understand very well. Once you finish your reading and jotting down the new words and phrases, take a few minutes to review these new words and phrases.

Read the reading for each lesson aloud and try to understand the general meaning of the reading text. You do not need to understand every single word, you just need to have a general idea.

Now you can view the Vocabulary section underneath the reading. Locate the words or phrases that you do not fully understand. Learn them by heart. You will also find remarks and notes indicating pages number where you can learn more about any structure that is not for this unit. Pay close attention to these remarks on the *Word List.*

Now, you are ready to listen the MP3 audio. Make sure you play the MP3 and listen to the pronunciation of the native speakers. Get the gist of the pronunciation and practice it. If possible, try to imitate the pronunciation for any possible word or phrase that you are not sure. Listen to the MP3 audio as many times as possible.

Once you master the **Words List** for this lesson,

you can now move to the **Grammar** section, stated by sign. Pay close attention to the words with the **Grammar** symbol. Review them in the text.

You are ready to move to the *A little bit more* section. In this section you will find list of phrases and / or new vocabularies to increase your learning skills. Make sure to learn them very well.

I have created a ***Knowledge Base*** section, where you will find basic information for each country where Spanish is the official language. Since there are 22 countries with Spanish as their official language, you will find a ***Knowledge Base*** on each lesson.

Your final and no less important section is "***Bible Verse***". I have included 22 Bible verses, one for each lesson, so you can conclude each lesson with a blessing and a Word from God to your heart. I have learned that there is no better resource to increase your learning skills and vocabulary as the "***Bible***". Try it and you will find words for every situation, occasion and time.

Make sure to repeat these steps over and over again until you master each lesson. Do not go to the next section if you have not mastered previous one. You MUST be sure you master each lesson before moving on. Your success will depend on following these steps.

Symbols And Abbreviations

Audio Symbol: This indicates that the MP3 Audio download is needed for this section

Dialogue Symbol: This indicates dialogue

Grammar Symbol: This indicates grammar explanations.

A little More Symbol: This indicates we have added a little more information to the lesson.

Lesson 1

Domingo Familiar – Family Sunday

Mi familia acostumbra reunirse todos los domingos. Vamos a la casa de la abuela y el abuelo. Allí *iríamos* todos: tíos., primos, yernos, nueras, mi papá y mi mamá, mi hermano y mi hermana y por supuesto yo. Los abuelos *disfrutarían* de tenernos cerca, especialmente a todos sus nietos.

La abuela sale de la cocina y anuncia: "El almuerzo ya casi está listo". Siempre tenemos *la mejor* de las comidas, la comida de mamá es buena, pero la de la abuela es *mejor.* Después de comer nos reunimos todos a hablar de nuestros planes, vamos a la sala, la habitación es relativamente pequeña pero cabemos todos. Nos encanta compartir pero hay algo malo que siempre terminamos discutiendo y peor aún los abuelos se *pondrían* bravos con todos. Gracias a Dios es fácil contentarlos, les basta un beso y un buen abrazo.

Hoy comienza a hablar María, es mi prima menor. María es la chica *más linda* de la clase, ella dice: "No tenía el valor de hablar con ustedes pero debo hacerlo, tuve una discusión con Omaira (mi hermana) esa mujer estaba completamente loca. Omaira es una embarcadora *acérrima*, me preguntó que *si me gustaría* salir con ella y nunca fue a buscarme".

Omaira se levanta de inmediato y dice: "Amiga mía eres *habladorsísima*, si fui pero te habías ido. *Hablaría* contigo pero estás enojada, además no *deberías* estar brava por mi impuntualidad, tú siempre llegas *tardísimo*".

El abuelo está bravo y dice: "Ya es suficiente, silencio".

Mamá interviene y cambia el tema, diciendo: "La comida estuvo *buenísima*.

La tía responde: "Estoy totalmente de acuerdo contigo. Por otra parte niñas recuerden que nosotros somos *los más inteligentes* del pueblo y no debemos estar discutiendo por cosas tan *misérrimas*".

No sé para qué papá volvió a tocar el tema. Ahora quien habla es Pedro, mi primo el hermano de María. Pedro es el chico *menos tranquilo* del grupo, dice señalando a mi hermana María: "Esta chica es *bellísima*, así que por eso es sumamente importante decirles lo qué pasó, pues Omaira no se atreve a decirlo. Saben que los jóvenes en su mayor parte no quieren estudiar, y aunque Santiago el compañero de Omaira es *el más inteligente* de la clase, él es absolutamente libérrimo, él se cree *mejor* que nosotros así que le escondió las llaves del auto a Omaira y por eso ella salió tan tarde a buscar a María.

María, arrepentida de lo que dijo se acerca a Omaira la abraza y le dice: "Perdóname prima, yo soy *menos fuerte que* tú y no soy *tan inteligente como* tú, no fui capaz de pensar que llegaste tarde, no porque quisiste sino porque no pudiste llegar más temprano.

El abuelo dice: ¿María por qué te consideras *menos*

inteligente y fuerte que los demás? Eres *celebérrima* por tu belleza y tu bondad, eres *la más atractiva* del grupo y eres *tan inteligente como* tu prima.

María le contesta llorando: Me siento mucho menos que los demás porque tengo un complejo de inferioridad.

Eso es más que suficiente para que toda la familia rodee a María y la llene de besos y abrazos que la hacen de nuevo sonreír. Otro domingo en familia que acaba lleno de alegría y unión familiar.

Word List – Listado de palabras
Domingo Familiar – Family Sunday.
Acostumbra reunirse - Have the custom to meet.
Y por supuesto yo – And of course me.
Hablar de nuestros planes – Speak about our plans.
Relativamente pequeña – Relatively small.
Pero hay algo malo – But there is something.
Siempre terminamos discutiendo – We alway end up arguing.
Se pondrían bravos – They would get upset (Bravos can be angry, upset or brave, fierce...)
No tenía el valor – Did not have the courage.
Completamente loca – Completely crazy.
Una embarcadora acérrima – A bitter humbug.
Habladorsísima – Super talkactive (In this sense, means a big lier).
Por mi impuntualidad – Because of my impunctuality.
Mamá interviene - Mom intervened.
Decirles lo qué pasó – Tell you what happened.
No se atreve a decirlo – She does not dare to say it.

En su mayor parte - Mostly.

Él se cree mejor que nosotros – He thinks he is better tan us.

Le escondió las llaves del auto -- He hid the keys of the car.

Perdóname prima – Forgive me cousin.

No fui capaz de pensar – I was not able to think.

Rodee a María - Surround Maria.

Y la llene de besos y abrazos – And fill her with kisses and hugs.

Que la hacen de nuevo sonreír – That makes her smile again.

Unión familiar – Family union.

Grammar Explanations – Notas gramaticales

Conditional Tense – Tiempo condicional.

It is very easy to conjugate the conditional tense *"Would"* in Spanish for all three-verb forms *"Ar / Er / Ir"*. It is used to talk about conditional or hypothetical events. They use the same endings; these endings are added on to the end of the infinitive. In other words, you take the verb as it is in Infinitive and just add the corresponding ending as shown below:

Hablar – Speak / Talk

Yo	hablar*ía*
Tú	hablar*ías*
Usted	hablar*ía*
Él	hablar*ía*
Ella	hablar*ía*

Nosotros	hablar*íamos*
Ustedes	hablar*ían*
Ellos (as)	hablar*ían*

Comer - Eat

Yo	comer*ía*
Tú	comer*ías*
Usted	comer*ía*
Él	comer*ía*
Ella	comer*ía*
Nosotros	comer*íamos*
Ustedes	comer*ían*
Ellos (as)	comer*ían*

Ir - Go

Yo	ir*ía*
Tú	ir*ías*
Usted	ir*ía*
Él	ir*ía*
Ella	ir*ía*
Nosotros	ir*íamos*
Ustedes	ir*ían*
Ellos (as)	ir*ían*

Remarks:

As you can see, the three groups of verbs have the same ending. Please note that all have accent in "í".

*Yo **hablar**ía contigo, pero no quiero hacerlo* – I would speak with you, but I don't want to do it.

*Ella **hablar**ía con él, pero ella está enojada* – She would talk to him, but she is angry.

*Nosotros **comer**íamos arroz con habichuela.* – We would eat rice and beans.

Would like - Gustaría

Gustaría – Would like. By using the conditional "would like" instead of the regular "want", you are more polite. We use the conditional to make polite requests or desires.

Me gustaría cenar contigo – I would like to have dinner with you.

¿Te gustaría salir conmigo? – Would you like to go out with me?

Si, me gustaría salir contigo. – Yes, I would like to go out with you.

No, no me gustaría salir contigo. – No, I would not like to go out with you.

¿Le gustaría a ella caminar con nosotros? – Would she like to walk with us?

Si, a ella le gustaría caminar con nosotros – Yes, she would like to walk with us.

No, a ella no le gustaría caminar con nosotros – No, she would not like to walk with us.

Nos gustaría dormir tranquilos esta noche. – We would like to sleep quite tonight.

¿Les gustaría un poco de café? – Would you (plural) like some coffee?

Si, nos gustaría un poco de café – Yes, we would like some coffee.

No, no nos gustaría un poco de café – No, we would not like coffee.

Remember to use the personal pronouns when you are referring to "*Usted / Él / Ella*" and "*Ustedes / Ellos (as)*".

Irregular verbs in the conditional tense – Verbos irregulares en el Condicional.

Every rule has its exceptions; therefore, here you have some irregular verbs in the conditional tense. You will notice the stem always end in "*R*" thus giving you the same sound to form the conditional for all verbs.

Caber – Fit	*cabr -*
Decir – Say / Tell	*dir -*
Hacer – Make / do	*har -*
Poder - Be able to / Can / May	*podr -*
Poner – Put -	*pondr -*
Querer – Want	*querr -*
Saber – Know	*sabr -*
Salir – Leave / Go out	*saldr -*
Tener – Have	*tendr -*
Valer - Be worth	*valdr -*
Venir – Come -	*vendr -*

Tener el valor de hablar con alguien – Have the courage to speak with someone.

Yo *tendría* el valor de hablar contigo. – I would have the courage to speak with you.

Tú *tendrías* el valor de hablar conmigo. – You would have the courage to speak with me.

Él *tendría* el valor de hablar con nosotros. – He would have the courage to speak with us.

Nosotros *tendríamos* el valor de hablar con ella. – We would have the courage to speak with her.

Ellas *tendrían* el valor de hablar con Él. – They would have the courage to speak with him.

We have already seen the Ask and Answer form above, just make sure you practice it. As a way of review, here you have the pattern.

¿Te gustaría ver una película hoy? – Would you like to watch a movie today?

*Si, **me gustaría** ver una película hoy.* – Yes, I would like to watch a movie today.

*No, no **me gustaría** ver una película hoy.* – No, I would not like to watch a movie today.

Short answers:
*Si, **me gustaría*** – Yes, I would.
*No, no **me gustaría*** – No, I wouldn't.

More Adverbs – Más adverbios
We have already seen a list of adverbs in Spanish; let us see some more below:

Mucho – Much / Many
*Tengo **muchos** deseos de verte* – I long to see you.

Tanto – So much / So many.
*Te extraño **tanto*** – I miss you so much.

Demasiado - Too much.
*Te quiero **demasiado*** – I love too much.

Muy poco - Very little.
*Pienso en ti **muy poco*** – I think of you very little.

Tan poco - So little.
*Sabes **tan poco** de la vida* – You know so Little about life.

Demasiado poco - Too little.
*Ganas **demasiado poco** dinero para pagar la renta* –

You earn too Little to pay the rent.

Casi – almost / nearly.
*El almuerzo está **casi** listo* – Lunch is almost ready.

Apenas – barely / scarcely.
***Apenas** puedo pagar la renta* – I can barely pay the rent.

Casi no / Apenas – hardly.
***Casi no** puedo hablar* – I can't hardly speak.

Para nada / en absoluto - not at all.
*No estoy **para nada** contento* – I am not happy at all.

Incluso / aún – even / Still.
***Aún** quiero aprender a bailar* – I still want to learn how to dance.

Aún más - even more.
*Ahora te amo **aún más*** – I love you even more now.

Aún menos - even less.
*Ahora te necesito **aún menos*** – I need you even less now.

Ni siquiera - not even.
***Ni siquiera** viniste a verme* – You did note even come to see me.

Parcialmente, a medias – partially.
El restaurante estaba parcialmente cerrado – The restaurant was partially closed.

En parte – partly.
En parte es tu culpa por dañar el carro – Partly it is your fault for breaking the car.

Enteramente – entirely.
Es enteramente tu responsabilidad arreglar la situación – It is entirely your responsability to fix the situation.

Completamente – completely.
Esa mujer estaba completamente loca – That woman was completely crazy.

Absolutamente – absolutely.
Estás absolutamente en lo cierto – You are absolutely right.

Relativamente – relatively.
La habitación es relativamente pequeña – The roo mis relatively small.

Al menos - at least.
Al menos viniste a comer hoy – At least you came to eat today.

Como máximo - at most.
Llegaré a casa como máximo a las 7 pm – I will be homre at most at 7 pm.

En gran parte – largely.
*La Republica Dominicana es **en gran parte** un país católico* - Dominican Republic is largely a Catholic country.

En su mayor parte – mostly.
***En su mayor parte** los jóvenes no quieren estudiar* – Mostly Young people don't want to study.

Principalmente – mainly.
*Estoy en casa **principalmente** los lunes* – I am at home mainling on Mondays.

Totalmente – totally.
*Estoy **totalmente** de acuerdo contigo* – I totally agree with you.

Sumamente – extremely.
*Es **sumamente** importante decirte lo que pasó* – It is extremely important to tell you what happened.

Tan – So.
*Estoy **tan** emocionado* – I am so excited.

Muy – very.
*Eres **muy** linda* – You are very pretty.

Demasiado – too.
*El precio es **demasiado** alto* – The Price is too high.

Suficiente – enough.
*Ya es **suficiente.** Silencio* – That's enough. Quiet.

Justo / apenas / sólo – just.

Sólo hazlo sin decir nada – Just do it without saying anything.

Sólo / solamente - only.

Ella solamente trataba de ayudarte – She was ony trying to help you.

As you may have seen, the ending *"ly"* in English is expressed by *"mente"* in Spanish. Easy, isn't it?

Comparative – Comparativo.

We are now going to learn how to compare things or person in Spanish. Comparatives are the comparison of one person or thing to another (*more, less,* or *as... as*).

Superiority - Superioridad

Más ... que   **More ... than (er... than).**

Yo soy más grande que tú – I am taller than you.

Ella es más inteligente que él – She is more intelligent tan him.

Nosotros somos más fuertes que ellos – We are stronger than them.

Más ... que denotes superiority over someone or something.

Inferiority - Inferioridad

Menos ... que   **less ... than (fewer ... than)**

Él es menos fuerte que ella – He is less strong than her.

Los carros son menos caros que los aviones - Cars are less expensive than plains.

*Historia es **menos** interesante **que** biología* – History is less interesting than biology.

Menos... que denotes inferiority below someone or something.

Equity - Igualdad
Tan... como   **as... as**

*Ella es **tan** inteligente **como** tú* – She is as intelligent as you.

*Nosotros somos **tan** honestos **como** ellos* – We are as honest as them.

*Tú eres **tan** feo **como** tu hermano* – You are as ugly as your brother.

Tanto ... como   as much as (as many as)
*Nosotros tenemos **tanto** dinero **como** ustedes* – We have as much money as you.

*Ella tiene **tantas** amigas **como** nosotros* – She has as many friends as us.

Tan... como and **Tanto... como** denote equity with someone or something. Tan... como is used with adjectives and adverbs. While **tanto** (tanta, tantos, tantas) is used with nouns and verbs.

Remarks:
With **más** and **menos**, the *que plus noun and / or pronoun construction* is optional. With **tan** and **tanto como**, however, the noun and / or pronoun is required.

Tanto must agree with gender and number (***tantos, tanta, tantas***).

adjectives – Adjetivos irregulares.

There are some irregular adjectives in the comparative.

Bueno – Good **mejor – better**

*Ellas son **mejores que** nosotros* – They are better than us.

*Estoy en **mejor** condición **que** tú* – I am in better shape than you.

Malo – bad **peor – worse**

*Ustedes son **peores que** ellos* – You are worst than them.

*Estás en **peor** condición **que** yo* – You are in worst shape than me.

Superlative – Superlativo.

The superlatives are formed with the "***definite article***" plus "***noun***" plus "***más***" or "***menos***" plus "***adjective***".

*María es **la chica más linda** de la clase* – Maria is the prettiest girl of the class.

*Pedro es **el chico menos tranquilo** del grupo* – Pedro is the least quiet boy in the Group.

*Soy **el más inteligente** de la clase* – I am the smartest of the class.

*Ella es **la menos atractiva** del grupo* – The is the least attractive of the group.

Remember, with the superlative everything must match with gender and number.

*Nosotros somos **los más inteligentes** del pueblo* – We are the smartest of the town.

El más inteligente – The most intelligent.

(Masculine singular)

Los más inteligentes – The most intelligents. (Masculine plural)

La más inteligente – The most intelligent. (Feminine singular)

Las más inteligentes – The most intelligents. (Feminine plural)

El menos interesante – The least interesting. (Masculine singular)

Los menos interesantes – The least interesting. (Masculine plural)

La menos interesante – The least interesting. (Feminine singular)

Las menos interesantes – The least interesting. (Feminine plural)

Irregular Superlative – Superlativo Irregular.

Bueno – Good

Mejor – Better

El mejor – The best

Malo – Bad

Peor – Worse

El peor – The worst.

Superlative with "ísimo (a)" – Superlativo con "ísimo (a)".

Did you know that you can also form a superlative by adding "*ísimo(s)*" or "*ísima(s)*" to an adjective and even some adverbs. This can mean as *very, really, extremely, super,* or any other *ultimate* word you can think of. Remember, it must match gender and number.

*Esa chica es **bellísima*** – That girl is the prettiest

one.

*La comida está **buenísima*** – The meal is the best.

*Estoy **encantadísimo** de conocerte* – I am extremely delighted to meet you.

*Tú siempre llegas **tardísimo*** – You always arrive super late.

*Excúsame, pero siempre estamos **ocupadísimos*** – Excuseme, but we are always super busy.

*Vas **despacísimo**, apresúrate* – You walk extremely slow, hurry.

Irregular form with "ísimo" – Forma irregular con "ísimo".

When the adjectives end in "*N / Dor / Or*", the suffix changes to "*Císimo / císima*".

Inferior - Inferior   Inferiorcísimo

*La calidad de tu trabajo es **inferiorcísimo*** – The quality of your work is the worst.

Hablador – Talkactive   Habladorcísimo

*Amigo mío, eres **habladorcísimo*** – My Friend, you talk too much. (In some Latin countries a "*Habladorcísimo*" is equivalent to a person who makes many fake stories and tell many lies. So, be careful when you use it.

Joven – Young   Jovencísimo

*Usted está **jovencísimo*** – You are super Young.

Many qualitative adjectives ending in "*r*" in their last syllable do not always take the "*ísimo / ísima*" ending, but instead replace the final "*r*" with "*érrimo/ érrima*".

Acre – Sour	*Acérrimo*
Célebre – Famous	*Celebérrimo*
Libre – Free	*Lebérrima*
Mísero - Stingy / Mean	*Misérrimo*
Salubre – Salubrious	*Salubérrima*

You will not see these words very often and a regular speaker does not handle this level of Spanish.

Do not forget the Ask and Answers form.

¿Eres tú el chico más inteligente de la clase? – Are you the most intelligent boy from the class?

Si, lo soy. – Yes, I am.

*Si, soy **el chico más inteligente** de la clase.* – Yes, I am the smartest boy of the class.

No, no lo soy. – No, I am not.

*No, no soy **el chico más inteligente** de la clase.* – No, I am not the smartest boy of the class.

¿Te consideras mucho más inteligente que yo? Do you consider yourself much more (far more) intelligent than me?

*Si, me creo **mucho más inteligente que** tú* – Yes, I consider myself more intellingent than you.

*No, no me creo **mucho más inteligente que** tú* – No, I don't consider myself much more (far more) intelligent than you.

¿Por qué te consideras mucho menos atractiva que las demás? Why do you consider yourself much less (far less) attractive than the rest?

Porque tengo complejo de inferioridad – Because I have low self-esteem.

A little bit more – Un poco más

The family   -   La Familia

Abuela	Grandmother
Abuelo	Grandfather
Bebé	Baby
Bisabuela	Great Grandmother
Bisabuelo	Great Grandfather
Cuñada	Sister in-law
Cuñado	Brother in-law
Hermana	Sister
Hermano	Brother
Hija	Daughter
Hijo	Son
Madre	Mother
Mamá	Mom
Nuera	Daughter in-law
Padre	Father
Papá	Dad
Primo / prima	Cousin
Suegra	Mother in-law
Suegro	Father in-law
Tatarabuela	Great Great Grandmother
Tatarabuelo	Great Great Grandfather
Tía	Aunt
Tío	Uncle
Yerno	Son in-law

Exercises - Ejercicios

1- Describe the following member of your family:

Teach Yourself Spanish Level Two

Tío_____

Primo _____

Bisabuela _____

Hermano_____

Mamá_____

Cuñado_____

2-   Write one sentence to describe what you would do if you: Win the lottery

_____

Travel to France

_____

Lose all your money

_____

Lose all your hair

_____

Meet your favorite actor/actress

_____

3- Complete the following sentences with comparative adjectives.

Tu mama es _____que tu papá.

El sol es _____que la tierra.

Mi hermana es _____como yo.

Dios es_____ que todos nosotros.

Un caballo es _____ como una vaca.

4- Write the superlatives for the following words:

Malo _____

Bueno _____

Grande _____

Gordo _____

Célebre _____

Reading Comprehension

¿Adónde voy los domingos? – Where do I go on Sundays?

¿Quiénes discutieron? – Who argued?

¿Cómo es la comida de mi abuela? – How is my grandmother's cooking?

Knowledge Base
Republic of Nicaragua - República de Nicaragua
Motto: En Dios confiamos - In God We Trust
Capital and largest city - Managua
Official language - Spanish

Recognized regional languages - *English, Miskito, Rama, Sumo, Miskito, Coastal, Creole, Garifuna, Rama, Cay Creole*

Demonym - Nicaraguans

Government - Unitary presidential constitutional republic

President - Daniel Ortega

Vice President - Omar Halleslevens

Population - 2016 census - 6 118 432

Currency - Córdoba (NIO)

Calling code - +505

Bible Verse - Versícuclo Bíblico

Porque la paga del pecado es muerte, más la dádiva de Dios es vida eterna en Cristo Jesús Señor nuestro. **Romanos 6:23**

Lesson 2
Vacación Tropical - Tropical Calling

Director: Los cité, *para* ante ustedes leer una noticia del Club Rotario Internacional. Según ellos los 10 mejores estudiantes de esta institución, realizarán un viaje como premio, y son: Roy, Brenda, Karla, Beatriz, Raúl, Andrés, Juan, Nancy, Olivia y Peter." Estudiar paga".

Roy: ¿Es en serio?

Director: Si, *saldrán* desde el 25 de junio y *estarán* de regreso el 09 de julio; por favor vayan a la agencia de viajes que está detrás de la Iglesia.

Carla: ¡Por Dios! ¿Nos *permitirán* viajar? Yo solo tengo 12 años, Raúl 14 y Peter 13

Director: vayan *para* la agencia con sus padres.

Andrés: este viaje vale oro para mí.

Beatriz: ¿Quién nos *guiará?*

Director: *Habrá* Paramédicos, Guarda Parques y Guías del Rotary.

Ted: ¿*Llevaremos* sacos para dormir?

Director: No es necesario.

Juan: *Para* entonces espero estar bien.

Olivia: *Saldremos* en 2 semanas.

Nancy: Ante todo *llevaremos* útiles personales, productos anti solares e hidratantes, toallas, cámaras fotográficas y de video y medicamentos quienes tienen tratamientos.

Director: Hay mucho entusiasmo. Mañana a las 8 a.m, en punto. ***Estaré*** aquí para hablar con sus representantes.

Profesor Miguel: señor director, los representantes llegaron.

Director: acompáñame. Buenos días, por motivo de ese viaje del que les informaron sus muchachos, los he citado, para hablar sobre él y aclarar dudas.

Señor Ruiz: ¿Cuánto cuesta?

Doctora Sofía: ¿A cuál país es el viaje?

Señora Rubio: ¿Irán solos?

Señora Sanders: ¿Cuántas hembras y varones ***viajarán?***

Director: Uno por uno, por favor. Nuestra institución fue escogida por el Club Rotario Internacional para participar en su programa de Intercambio Vacacional de Ecoturismo, están premiando a los mejores 10 estudiantes con un viaje a un país tropical: *Venezuela*. Por casualidad van 5 hembras y 5 varones, no ***costará*** ni un centavo; deben llevar ropa ligera, trajes de baño, 2 pares de zapatos cómodos, aun siendo tropical ***van a*** visitar un sitio muy frio, deben llevar ropa de invierno e incluir un impermeable para usarlo en las zonas lluviosas, lleven gorras, protector solar, repelente para mosquitos y linternas. No ***irán*** solos, Miguel el profesor de deportes los ***acompañará***. Pasen por la agencia de Viajes para tener todo listo a tiempo. Por aquí hay unas planillas para que las llenen y las firmen dando su aprobación por escrito. En el anexo desprendible ***van a*** colocar el nombre de la representante que desean vaya acompañando a los chicos, tras escribirlo colocar el desprendible doblado sobre esta bandeja.

Profesor Miguel: yo *voy a* contar los votos, hay 9 para la doctora Sofía y uno más que dice "Yo quiero ir", por supuesto el último es nulo.

Director: Estoy empezando a pensar que quieren un médico en el grupo, por ventura están a cargo de ahora en delante de este viaje dos estupendos chaperones: el profesor Miguel y la doctora Sofía, entre sus deberes está el de ir reportando diariamente, por correo electrónico o por teléfono.

Doctora Sofía: lo haremos todas las noches.

Director: Hoy es 25 de junio, hoy *vas a* viajar con el grupo a Venezuela,

Profesor Miguel: por lo visto están todos aquí tanto alumnos como representantes, desde las 7:00 a.m.

Director: Son tal para cual.

Profesor Miguel: *vamos a* salir ya, siendo un vuelo internacional debemos estar por lo menos 3 horas antes, por si acaso. Salgamos en caravana vía aeropuerto.

Doctora Sofía: Bueno, despídanse ya *vamos a* entrar los 13.

Director: ¿Trece?

Doctora Sofía: Si, Diosito nos acompaña.

Word List – Listado de palabras
Vacación Tropical – Tropical Vocation (calling).
Los cité – I called you.
Según ellos – According to them.
De esta institución – From this institution.

Un viaje como premio – A trip as a reward.

Estudiar paga – Studying pays.

Y estarán de regreso – And you will be back.

Agencia de viajes – Travel agency.

¡Por Dios! - My Gosh.

Este viaje vale oro para mí – This trip worths gold.

Habrá –There will be.

Útiles personales – Personal items.

Productos anti solares - Sun blockers.

Sus representantes – Your representatives.

Acompáñame – Accompany me.

Aclarar dudas. – Clear doubts.

Hembras y varones - Females and males.

Programa de Intercambio Vacacional – Vacational Exchange program.

Ecoturismo – Eco-Tourism.

Están premiando – They are rewarding.

No costará ni un centavo – It will cost nothing.

Deben llevar ropa ligera – You should take light clothes.

Zonas lluviosas – Rainy zones.

Repelente para mosquitos – Mosquito's repelent.

Linternas –Flash lights.

Unas planillas para que las llenen – Some forms to fill out.

Aprobación por escrito – Written approval.

Anexo desprendible – Tear up page.

Colocar el desprendible doblado – Place the folded paper.

Sobre esta bandeja – On a tray.

Contar los votos – Count votes.

Por ventura – Hopefully (Luckily).

Dos estupendos chaperones – Two amazing chaperones.

Entre sus deberes - Among their duties.

Reportando diariamente – Report on a daily basis.

Por correo electrónico – By email.

Por lo visto – As we can see.

Por si acaso – Just in case.

Salgamos en caravana vía aeropuerto

Despídanse – Say firewell (Good-bye).

Diosito nos acompaña. – God be with us. (*Diosito is a diminutive use in this case, for God, but not as diminutive, rather as tender and showing pleading to God.* See lesson 21)

Grammar Explanations – Notas gramaticales

Prepositions in Spanish. – Preposiciones en español.

Prepositions indicate the relationship between words or linking them together. They can show location, direction and time. In Spanish, there are simple prepositions "one word" and compound prepositions "multiple words".

Simple Prepositions – Preposiciones simples.

Below you will find a list of the most common simple prepositions in Spanish.

*A	to / at
Ante	before / in the presence of
Bajo / abajo / debajo	under
Con	with
Contra	against

*De	**of / from**
Desde	from / since
Detrás de	behind
*En	**in / on / at**
Entre	between / among
Hacia	toward
Hasta	until / toward
*Para	**for / in order to**
*Por	**for / by**
Según	according to
Sin	without
Sobre	about / on / upon / above / over / around
Tras / atrás / detrás	after / behind

Remarks:

*A   **to / at**

Indicating motion "to"

Vamos a Paris – Let us go to Paris.

Vamos al restaurante el miércoles – Let us go to the restaurant on Wednesday.

When you use the preposition "*A*" together with the article "*El*", they have a contract form "*a+el = Al*". Vamos al *(a +el)* restaurant – Let's go to the restaurant.

Connecting a verb with the infinitive.

Empiezo a pensar – I start to think.

Vamos a dormir – Let us go to sleep.

Indicating how something is done "on – by - with"

Lo hice a mano – I made by hand.

Vamos a pie – Let us go on foot.

Vamos a escribir a lápiz – Let us write with a pencil.

Introducing a person as a direct object.

¿Conoces a Pedro? – Do you know Pedro?

Te presento a Carlos – I introduce you to Carlos.

¿Ves a mi hermana? – Do you see my sister?

Expressing time "at"

El desayuno es a las siete (7:00 am) – Breakfast is at 7:00 am.

Estamos a diez y seis de Julio – It is July 16th.

*De   of / from

As we have already learned, in indicates possession "De – of"

El carro de Pedro – Pedro's car / the car of Pedro.

Indicating cause "from / with".

Estamos cansados de caminar – We are tired from caminar.

Estoy contento de mi trabajo – I am happy with my work.

Indicating origin "from / of"

Nosotros somos de Italia – We are from Italy.

Yeiris es la más hermosa de la clase – Yeiris is the most beautiful of the class.

When you use the preposition "***De - From***" together with the article "***El***", they have a contract form "***de+el = Del***". Vengo del *(de +el)* restaurant – I come from the restaurant.

Describing a noun with another noun or infinitive "of"

Un vaso de agua – A glass of water.
Un copa de vino – A cup of wine.
Un jugo de limón – A lemon juice.

Some idiomatic expressions

Estoy de pie – I am standing.
De ahora en adelante – From now on.
*En   in / on / at

Indicating location "in / on / at"

El dinero está en mi cartera – The money is in my wallet.

El vaso está en la mesa – The glass is on the table.

Nosotros estamos en la iglesia – We are at the church.

Indicatin time "in"

Voy a la iglesia en una hora – I am going to church in an hour.

Voy al campo en el verano – I go to my hometown in the summer.

Indicating how something is done "by"

Voy al cine en autobús – I go to the movies by bus.

Vamos a la Universidad en carro – We go to the university by car.

In some idiomatic expression

El espectáculo es en vivo – The show is live.
¿Es en serio? – Are you serious?
Es en broma – I am joking.

Pay special attention to what is considered one of the hardest things to learn in Spanish **"Por / Para"**. I am giving you specific guidelines for you to master the American headache. At the end of this section, you will see that is not that difficult, as peope tend to think.

The preposition "Para" shows.
Destination and place
Salgo para la iglesia – I am leaving for church.
Salimos para la ciudad – We are leaving to the city.

Destination and person
Este regalo es para Ella – This gift is for her.
Aquellas manzanas en la mesa son para nosotros – Those apples over there on the table are for us.

A future time limit
El trabajo es para mañana – The job is for tomorrow.
El bizcocho es para esta noche – The cake is for tonight.

Purpose and goal
Estudio para aprender – I study to learn.
Bailo para divertirme – I dance to have fun.

Use and function
Es una pastilla para el dolor de cabeza – It is a pill for the headache.
Es un cepillo para cepillarse – It is a brush to brush your teeth.

Comparisons

Para la edad de Ella, se ve muy bien – For her age, she looks very well.

Para la edad de nosotros, trabajamos demasiado – For our age, we work too much.

Opinions

، *Para nosotros es demasiado tarde* – It is too late for us.

Para mí es demasiado amargo – It is too sour for me.

Some expressions with "Para"

¿Para qué?   why? for what purpose?

¿Para qué quieres el dinero? – For what purpose do you need the money?

Para comprar un coche Nuevo – To buy a new car.

Estar para   **to be about to**

No estoy para hablar – I am not about to talk.

Para adelante   **forward**

Siempre vamos para adelante – We are always going forward.

Para atrás   **backward**

No entiendo por qué siempre vas para atrás en vez de ir para adelante. – I don't understand why you are always going backward instead of going forward.

Para entonces   **by that time (By then).**

Estaré en casa para entonces – I will be home by that time.

Para esa época   **by that time**

Para esa época éramos muy pobres y no teníamos que comer – By that time, we are so por and we did not have what to eat.

ara otra vez   **for another occasion**

No se pudo hoy, para otra vez será – It was not possible today, it will be for another occasion.

Para que   **so that, in order that**

Para que puedas aprender, tienes que estudiar – In order to learn you have to study.

Para siempre   **forever**

Estaré en deuda contigo para siempre – I will always be in debt with you.

Para variar   **just for a change**

Vamos a la playa para variar – Let us go go the beach just for a change.

Ser tal para cual   **be two of a kind**

Mi padre y yo somos tal para cual – My father and I are two of a kind.

The preposition "Por" shows.
Motion and place

Caminamos por las calles de Paris – we walk through the streets of Paris.

Andamos por las tiendas de Nueva York – We walk through the stores of New York.

Means and manner

Te envío la invitación por email. – I send you the invitation by email.

Necesito el paquete aquí. Te lo envío por correo postal. – I need the package here. I will send it by mail.

In exchange for and substitution

Sabemos que no debemos, pero vamos a hacerlo por Carlos – we know we should not to, but we will do it for Carlos.

No quiero, pero por ti lo haré – I don't want, but I will do it for you.

Duration of an action

Hago ejercicios por dos horas – I do exercices for two hours.

Me siento en la computadora por 12 horas – I sit on the computer for twelve hours.

Indefinite time period

Descanso por la mañana – I rest in the morning.

Trabajo por las noches – I work at night.

On behalf of

María hablará en la conferencia por mí – Maria is going to speak at the conference for me.

No puedo beber cerveza. Está bien, yo me la bebo por ti. – I cannot drink beer. It is ok, I will drink it for you.

Per

Me pagan por hora – I get paid per hour.

Nos pagan por día – We get paid per day.

Some expressions with the preposition "Por" – Algunas expresiones con "Por".

¡Por Dios! Oh my God!	For heaven's sake!
Día por día	Day by day
Palabra por palabra	Word by word
Por adelantado	In advance
Por ahora	For now
Por amor de Dios	For the love of God
Por aquí	This way
Por casualidad	By chance
Por ciento	Percent
Por cierto	Certainly

Por completo	completely
Por correo	By mail / post
Por dentro	Inside
Por desgracia	Unfortunately
Por ejemplo	For example
Por escrito	In writing
Por eso	Therefore, that's why
Por favor	Please
Por fin	Finally
Por la mañana, la tarde, la noche	
	In the morning, afternoon, evening
Por las buenas o por las malas	
	Whether you like it or not
Por lo demás	Furthermore
Por lo general	Generally, in general
Por lo menos	At least
Por lo mismo	For that very reason
Por lo que a mí me toca	As far as I'm concerned
Por lo que he oído	Judging by what I've heard
Por lo tanto	Therefore
Por lo visto	Apparently
Por malo que sea...	However bad it is...
Por medio de	By means of
Por motivo de	On account of
Por ningún lado	Nowhere
Por otra parte	On the other hand
Por poco	Almost
Por primera	For the first
Por separado	Separately
Por si acaso	Just in case
Por su propia mano	By one's own hand
Por suerte	Fortunately

Por supuesto	Of course
Por teléfono	On the phone / by phone
Por todas partes	Everywhere
Por todos lados	On all sides
Por última vez	For the last time
Por último	Finally
Una vez por todas	Once and for all

Compound prepositions – Preposiciones compuestas.

Compound Prepositions are used mostly by native speakers and are generally made up of **preposition + noun + preposition** or **adverb + preposition.**

A cargo de	in charge of.
A causa de	because of / due to.
A excepción de	with exception of.
A favor de	in favor of.
A fines de	at the end of.
A mediados de	around.
A pesar de	in spite of.
A través de	through.
Acerca de	concerning.
Además de	moreover.
Al norte de	to the north of.
Al sur de	to the south of.
A través de	across from.
Alrededor de	around.
Antes de	before.
Cerca de	close to.
Contrario a	contrary to.
De ahora en adelante	from now on.

More Irregular verbs in the present tense – Más verbos irregulares en el presente.

Discernir lo verdadero de lo falso – Discern real from fake (Distinguish).

Yo *discierno lo verdadero de lo falso* – I discern real from fake.

Tú *disciernes lo verdadero de lo falso* – You discern real from fake.

Usted / *Él* / Ella *discierne lo verdadero de lo falso* – He discerns real from fake.

Nosotros *discernimos lo verdadero de lo falso* – We discern real from fake.

Ustedes / *Ellos* (as) *disciernen lo verdadero de lo falso* – They discern real from fake.

Oler una aroma exquisita – Smell an exquisite scent.

Yo *huelo una aroma exquisita* – I smell an exquisite scent.

Tú *hueles una aroma exquisita* – You smell an exquisite scent.

Usted / Él / *Ella* *huele una aroma exquisita* – She smells an exquisite scent.

Nosotros *olemos una aroma exquisita* – We smell an exquisite scent.

Ustedes / *Ellos* (as) *huelen una aroma exquisita* – They smell an exquisite scent.

Pay special attention to the conjugation of "nosotros".

Satisfacer la curiosidad de las personas – Satisfy the curiosity of people.

Yo *satisfago la curiosidad de las personas* – I satisfy the curiosity of people.

Tú *satisfaces la curiosidad de las personas* – You satisfy the curiosity of people.

Usted / Él / Ella *satisface la curiosidad de las personas* – He satisfies the curiosity of people.

Nosotros *satisfacemos la curiosidad de las personas* – We satisfy the curiosity of people.

Ustedes / **Ellos** (as) *satisfacen la curiosidad de las personas* – They satisfy the curiosity of people.

Valer oro – Be worth gold.

Yo *valgo oro* – I am worth gold.

Tú *vales oro* - You are worth gold.

Usted / Él / **Ella** *vale oro* – She is worth gold.

Nosotros *valemos oro* – We are worth gold.

Ustedes / **Ellos** (as) *valen oro* – They are worth gold.

Caber en la caja – Fit in the box.

Yo *quepo en la caja* – I fit in the box.

Tú *cabes en la caja* – You fit in the box.

Usted / **Él** / Ella *cabe en la caja* – He fits in the box.

Nosotros *cabemos en la caja* – We fit in the box.

Ustedes / **Ellos** (as) *caben en la caja* – They fit in the box.

Going to "Ir + A" – Futuro Próximo.

How to use "**Going to**" in Spanish. It is quite easy and simple, in fact you have already learned in a subtle way. We are going to speak about it. We form this time by using the present conjugation of the verb "**Ir**" *plus* "**A**" plus the infinitive of the verb indicating the action. Do you remember how to conjugate "Ir"? Of course, you do. Let us see below.

Yo	voy
Tú	vas
Usted	va
Él	va
Ella	va
Nosotros	vamos
Ustedes	van
Ellos (as)	van

Ir a comer – Going to eat.

*Yo **voy a comer** –* I am going to eat.

*Tú **vas a estudiar** –* You are going to study.

*Usted **va a cantar** –* You (polite) are going to sing.

*Él **va a cocinar** –* He is going to cook.

*Ella **va a trabajar** –* She is going to work.

*Nosotros **vamos a viajar** –* We are going to travel.

*Ustedes **van a nadar** –* You (plural) are going to swim.

*Ellos (as) **van a pescar** –* They are going to fish.

Easy, isn't it? You already knew how to speak in future tense. You just need to think on the verb or the action you want to do that "voilà".

Do not forge the Ask and Answer form.

¿Van ustedes a nadar? – Are you going to swim?

*Si, nosotros **vamos a nadar**.* – Yes, we are going to swim.

*No, nosotros no **vamos a nadar**.* – No, we are not going to swim.

¿Vamos nosotros a viajar? – Are we going to travel?

*Si, nosotros **vamos a viajar**.* – Yes, we are going to travel.

*No, nosotros no **vamos a viajar**.* – No, we are not

going to travel.

¿Va ella a trabajar? – Is she going to work?

Si, ella va a trabajar. – Yes, she is going to work.

No, ella no va a trabajar. – No, she is not going to work.

¿Vas tú a estudiar? – Are you going to study?

Si, yo voy a estudiar. – Yes, I am going to study.

No, yo no voy a estudiar. – No, I am not going to study.

Remarks:

As always to avoid confusion it is good to use the personal pronoun when referring to "*Usted / Él / Ella*" and "*Ustedes / Ellos (as)*".

You can obmit the pronouns with referring to "*I, You*", *We*".

¿Vas a trabajar mañana? – Are you going to work tomorrow?

Si, voy a trabajar mañana. Yes, I am going to work tomorrow.

No, no voy a trabajar mañana. No, I am not going to work tomorrow.

¿Vamos a cenar mañana? – Are we going to dine tomorrow?

Si, vamos a cenar mañana. – Yes, we are going to dine tomorrow.

No, no vamos a cenar mañana. – No, we are not going to dine tomorrow.

When using the short form in question for "nosotros", I strongly suggest you to use the pronoun "nosotros" to show that it is a question (in written form) and if it is speaking, then make sure you use the correct intonation denoting a question. See why:

Vamos a cenar mañana – Let us dine tomorrow.

¿Vamos a cenar mañana? Are we going to dine tomorrow?

As you can see, it is the same in both sentences. The only thing that will make the difference when speaking is your intonation and when writing using "*nosotros*".

¿Vamos notros a cenar mañana? – Are we going to dine tomorrow?

Future tense – Tiempo futuro.

It is the easiest time to use and construct in Spanish as you will see. 90% of the time, you can speak without even using the future, but it is very important the learn it, because you will indeed use it. El "*Futuro – Future*" is used for upcoming events. It is usually translated as "*will*".

It is the same for the three conjugations and guess what? You don't even have to worry about taking off the "*Ar / Er / Ir*" ending. *To form the future tense of -AR, -ER, and -IR verbs, add the appropriate ending to the infinitive.*

Hablar	–	Speak / Talk
Yo		hablar*é*
Tú		hablar*ás*
Usted		hablar*á*
Él		hablar*á*
Ella		hablar*á*
Nosotros		hablar*emos*
Ustedes		hablar*án*
Ellos (as)		hablar*án*

Comer	–	Eat
Yo		comer*é*
Tú		comer*ás*
Usted		comer*á*
Él		comer*á*
Ella		comer*á*
Nosotros		comer*emos*
Ustedes		comer*án*
Ellos (as)		comer*án*
Ir	-	go
Yo		ir*é*
Tú		ir*ás*
Usted		ir*á*
Él		ir*á*
Ella		ir*á*
Nosotros		ir*emos*
Ustedes		ir*án*
Ellos (as)		ir*án*

Remarks:

As you can see, it also works with irregular verbs. Of course, there are irregular verbs in the future by changing the stem, but the ending will always be the same.

Hablaré contigo el lunes – I will speak with you on Monday.

Cenaremos el Viernes a las 7 pm – We will dine on Friday at 7 pm.

Ella partirá para los Estados Unidos mañana – She will leave to The United States tomorrow.

Do not forget the Ask and Answers form.

¿Hablarás conmigo mañana? – Will you speak with me tomorrow?

Si, hablaré contigo mañana. – Yes, I will speak with you tomorrow.

No, no hablaré contigo mañana. – No, I will not speak with you tomorrow.

Irregular verbs in the future – Verbos irregulares en el futuro.

Some irregular verbs in the future. They still use the same endings as regular verbs. You will see that the stem always ends in *"R"*, and that these are the exact same as the irregular conditional stems.

Caber - Fit it		*cabr-*
Decir	- Say / Tell	*dir-*
Haber – Exist / Have		*habr-*
Hacer	- Do / Make	*har-*
Oír – Listen / Hear		*oir-*
Poder	- Can / May	*podr-*
Poner	- Put	*pondr-*

These verbs follow the same pattern as *"Poner"* componer - *Compose, disponer - Dispose, imponer - Impose, proponer - Propose, reponerse - Recover, suponer - Suppose.*

Querer – Want	*querr-*
Reír – Laugh	*reir- **

It follows the same patter as *"Reir"* sonreír – *Smile.*

Saber – Know	*sabr-*
Salir – Go out	*saldr-*
Tener	- Have	*tendr-*

These verbs follow the same patter as *"Tener"* contener - *Contain, detener - Detain, mantener – Maintain / Keep, obtener – Obtain / Get, retener – Retain / Withhold.*

Valer – Be worth   *valdr-*
Venir   - Come   *vendr-*

Remarks
Decir   **la verdad - Say / Tell the truth.**
Yo *Diré la verdad.* – I will tell the truth.
Tú *Dirás la verdad.* – You will tell the truth.
Usted / Él / Ella   *Dirá la verdad.* – You (polite) / He / She will tell the truth.
Nosotros   *Diremos la verdad.* – We will tell the truth.
Ustedes / Ellos (as)   *Dirán la verdad.* – You (plural) / They will tell the truth.

A little bit more – Un poco más

El clima / La temperatura - The weather.

Está nevando	It is snowing
Está lloviendo	It is raining
Está nublado	It is cloudy
Hay neblina	It is foggy
Hay una brisa	There is a breeze
Hay viento	It is windy
Hay mucho viento	It is very windy
Hay sol	It is sunny
Hay frio / Hace frio	It is cold
Hay fresco / Hace fresco	It is cool
Hay calor / Hace calor	It is warm/ It is hot
Está húmedo	It is humid
El cielo esta despajado	The sky is clear
Tormenta	Storm

Granizo	Hail
Temperatura	Temperature
Nieve	Snow
Lluvia	Rain
Llovizna	Light rain / drizzle
Un aguacero	Heavy rain / rainstorm
Llover a cantaros	Raining cats and dogs
Viento	Wind
Tornado	Tornado
Huracán	Hurricane
Mal tiempo	Bad weather
Buen tiempo	Good weather
Un trueno	Thunder
Un relámpago	A lightning flash
Un rayo	Ray of lightning
Inundación	Flood
Escarcha	Frost
El sereno	Dew

Exercises - Ejercicios

1- Write a list of 10 simple prepositions.

2- Write a sentence indication motion "to"

_____

3- Write a sentence connecting a verb with the infinitive.

_____

4- Write a sentence indicating how something is done "on-by-with".

_____

5- Write a sentence introducing a person as a direct object.

_____

6- Write a sentence expressing time "at-is".

_____

7- Write a sentence indicating location "in-on-at".

_____

8- Write a sentence indicating time "in"

_____

9- Write a sentence indicating how something is done "by".

_____

10- Write a sentence in some idiomatic expression.

_____

11- Write a sentence indicating destination and place.

_____

12- Write a sentence indicating destination and person.

_____

13- Write a sentence indicating a future time limit.

_____

14- Write a sentence indicating purpose and goal.

_____

15- Write a sentence indicating use and function.

_____

16- Write a sentence indicating comparison.

17- Write a sentence indicating opinions.

18- Write 3 sentences indicating some expressions with "para".

---

19 The preposition "POR"
Write a sentence indicating motion and place.

Write a sentence indicating means and manner.

Write a sentence indicating in exchange for and substitution.

Write a sentence indicating duration of an action.

Write a sentence indicating indefinite time.

Write a sentence indicating on behalf of.

---

20   Some expressions with preposition "POR"
Write 3 sentences using expressions of preposition "POR".

_____

_____

_____

21   Compound prepositions
Write 2 sentences using
preposition+noun+preposition.

_____

_____

22   Write 2 sentences using adverb+preposition

_____

_____

23   Going to   ir+a   Next future.

Write 2 sentences using Next future.

_____

24 Ask and Answer form.

Write 2 pairs of sentences using the ask and answer form.

_____

_____

25 Future Tense

Conjugate 1 regular verb in future tense.

_____

26 Conjugate 1 irregular verb in the future tense.

_____

27 Ask and answer form in future tense.

Write 2 pairs of sentences using the ask and answer form in future tense.

_____

_____

28 Irregular verbs in the future

Conjugate 2 irregular verbs in the future tense.

_____

_____

29 The Weather and the Temperature

Write a ten words list indicating weather or temperature.

_____

_____

Knowledge Base
Republic of Costa Rica - República de Costa Rica
Capital and largest city - San José
Official language - Spanish
Recognized regional languages – Mekatelyu, Bribri, Patois
Demonym - Costa Rican Tico
Government - Unitary presidential constitutional republic
President - Luis Guillermo Solís
1st Vice-President - Helio Fallas Venegas
2nd Vice-President - Ana Helena Chacón Echeverría
Population - 2015 census - 4 836 438
Currency - Costa Rican colón (CRC)
Calling code - +506
Bible Verse - Versículo Bíblico
He aquí, yo estoy a la puerta y llamo; si alguno oye mi voz y abre la puerta, entraré a él, y cenaré con él, y él conmigo. **Apocalipsis 3:20**

Lesson 3

¿Te Apetece un Habano? - Would you like a Cuban cigar?

Cuando Cristóbal Colón **descendió** de sus barcos y **pisó** tierras cubanas los indígenas le **dieron** como presente un montón de hojas secas, que eran desconocidas para él, lo que hoy conocemos como tabaco.

¿Qué **ocurrió** *con el tabaco?*

A partir de ese momento la planta del tabaco recorre el mundo y la gente se apasiona con él.

En Cuba, el rey Felipe V **impuso** en 1717 un monopolio real del tabaco y este *era* cultivado por hombres libres, de allí en adelante nace el campesino cubano, quien hoy día sigue cultivando esta planta.

¿Cómo se le Conoce?

Es conocido como el Habano, debe su nombre a la bella ciudad cubana de la Habana. Aunque otros tabacos se hacen pasar por habanos, los únicos y verdaderos son los que provinieron del tabaco que se **cultivó** en Cuba y que fueron manufacturados en ese país.

¿Por qué los Amantes del Tabaco Prefieren los Habanos?

La calidad del habano se ha debido siempre a cuatro elementos:

El clima, Cuba tiene un clima húmedo y caluroso que favorece el cultivo de la planta del tabaco.

El suelo, el suelo rojo y rico en níquel de Cuba es propicio para el tabaco.

El campesino cubano: Estos hombres **sembraron** tabaco desde siempre, desde antes inclusive de la llegada de los españoles, la sabiduría corre por sus venas.

Variedad: El tabaco cubano tiene múltiples aromas y sabores, siempre sorprende al que lo fuma.

¿Cómo se **crearon** *los Tabacos que tanto amas?*

El cultivo **comenzó** en el semillero, que es donde se **pusieron** las semillas para que germinasen.

Luego se **trasladó** la semilla al campo, y allí se quedó por 40 días.

Después se **recolectó** la hoja y se **llevó** a los lugares de ensarte.

Ya ensartadas las hojas se **llevaron** en carreta o a caballo hasta las galeras para que se sequen.

Le **quitaron** la vena central a la hoja y las **clasificaron.**

Las hojas se **fermentaron** y **estuvieron** listas.

Entonces fueron llevadas a un torcedor, se las llevan en carro o camión. Un torcedor es el que **escogió** la mezcla de hojas de tu habano y es quien las **torció** para crearlo.

Después se **añejó** de nuevo por más tiempo y por último se les **empaquetó** en su típica caja de cedro.

Por último se **llevaron** en trenes, barcos y aviones a todas partes del mundo.

La Habana es famosa por su música y hermosas mujeres pero, ¿quién no oyó hablar del célebre habano cubano?

Word List – Listado de palabras

¿Te Apetece un Habano? – Would you like a Habano (Cuban cigar)?

Descendió de sus barcos - Descended of his ships.

Tierras cubanas – Cuban lands

Los indígenas - The Indians

Como presente – As a present.

Un montón de hojas secas – A bunch of dry leaves.

Que eran desconocidas para él – That were unknown to him.

A partir de ese momento - From that momento on.

La planta del tabaco - Tabacco's tree.

Un monopolio real – A royal monopoly.

Era cultivado – It was cultivated.

Nace el campesino cubano – Cuban countryman is born.

Es conocido como el Habano – It is known as the Habano.

Se hacen pasar – They are passed.

Y que fueron manufacturados – And that were manufactured.

Cuatro elementos – Four elements.

Clima húmedo y caluroso – Humid and warm temparature.

Rico en níquel - Rich in nickel.

Es propicio - It is fit (good for).

Desde siempre – Since always.

La sabiduría corre por sus venas – Wisdom runs through their veines.

Siempre sorprende al que lo fuma – It always

surprises smoker.

El semillero – The seeadbed.

Las semillas para que germinasen. – The sedes to germinate.

Los lugares de ensarte – Thread places.

La vena central – Central vein

Un torcedor – A twister (Spindler).

Se añejó de nuevo – Be mature again.

Su típica caja de cedro. – Its typical cedar box.

📓 **Grammar Explanations – Notas gramaticales**

🔒 **Simple past or Preterit – Pasado simple o Pretérito.**

When you are referring to completed actions, when the verb refers to an action that has a clear end. You use the Preterit form in Spanish.

As you already learned there are three groups of verbs, however, the conjugation for the second and third group is the same.

Hablar	Speak / Talk.
Yo	habl*é*
Tú	habl*aste*
Usted	habl*ó*
Él	habl*ó*
Ella	habl*ó*
Nosotros	habl*amos*
Ustedes	habl*aron*
Ellos (as)	habl*aron*

Hablé con Sara del problema – I spoke with Sara about the problem.

Hablamos con Pedro de la situación – We spoke

with Pedro about the situation.

We use the Preterit when something happened once.

Ayer hablé con Sara – I spoke with Sara yesterday.

Caminé 4 kilómetros ayer – I walked four kilometers yesterday.

When something happened more than once, but had a specific end.

Ella trabajó 60 horas la semana pasada – She worked 60 hours last week.

Él cantó sin parar en su último concierto – He sang non-stopping on his last concert.

When indicating the beginning and end of a process.

La tormenta terminó a media noche – The storm ended at midnight.

El sol se paró a medio día – The sun stopped at midday.

Remarks:

As you can see, all these actions had an end. They happened once and those that happened more than once had a specific end.

Notice the accent on the first person "**hablé**" and third person singular "**habló**". Make sure you use the accent, because it can make the difference when speaking.

Hablo español contigo – I speak Spanish with you.

Habló español contigo – He spoke Spanish with you.

The conjugation for "Nosotros" in the Preterit is the same for the simple present.

Nosotros hablamos – We speak (simple present)

Nosotros hablamos – We spoke (Preterit).

Do not panic; just remember that the Preterit indicates an action that took time in the past and had an end. That will ease your mind.

Do not forget the Ask and Answers form.

¿Hablaste con Pedro ayer? – Did you speak with Pedro yesterday?

Si, hablé con Pedro ayer. – Yes, I spoke with Pedro yesterday.

No, no hablé con Pedro ayer. – No, I did not speak with Pedro yesterday.

¿Por qué él trabajó sólo en el proyecto? – Why did he work alone in the Project?

Él trabajó sólo en el proyecto porque nadie lo entiende – He worked alone in the Project because none understands him.

Preterit for "Er" and "Ir" Verbs – Pretérito de los verbos "Er / Ir"

The Preterit for "Er" and "Ir" verbs is the same and the use of the time is the same as explained above.

Comer – Eat		Salir – Go out
Yo	com*í*	sal*í*
Tú	com*iste*	sal*iste*
Usted	com*ió*	sal*ió*
Él	com*ió*	sal*ió*
Ella	com*ió*	sal*ió*
Nosotros	com*imos*	sal*imos*
Ustedes	com*ieron*	sal*ieron*
Ellos (as)	com*ieron*	sal*ieron*

*Me **levanté**, me **vestí**, y **salí** para la iglesia* - I got up, got dressed, and left for church.

Entraste, ***bebiste*** *un vaso de jugo, y* ***comiste*** *una manzana.* - *You* ***came in, drank*** *a glass of juice, and* ***ate*** *an apple.*

Irregular verbs in the Preterit form – Verbos irregulares en el Pretérito.

Dar – Give	Ser – Be	
Yo	di	fui
Tú	diste	fuiste
Usted	dio	fue
Él	dio	fue
Ella	dio	fue
Nosotros	dimos	fuimos
Ustedes	dieron	fueron
Ellos (as)	dieron	fueron

Ir	–	Go
Yo		fui
Tú		fuiste
Usted		fue
Él		fue
Ella		fue
Nosotros		fuimos
Ustedes		fueron
Ellos (as)		fueron

Él me ***dio*** *un regalo de cumpleaños* – He gave me a birthday present.

Yo ***fui*** *profesor en la secundaria* – I was a high school teacher.

Yo ***fui*** *a Portugal el año pasado* – I went to Portugal last year.

If you noticed, **"Ser" and "Ir"** share the exact same

conjugation in the Preterit. Even they have the same exact conjugation, as you can see; it is easy to differentiate the meaning. Please note that there was no accent with these verbs in the Preterit.

Andar – Walk	Estar – Be	Tener - Have
Anduve	Estuve	Tuve
Anduviste	Estuviste	Tuviste
Anduvo	Estuvo	Tuvo
Anduvimos	Estuvimos	Tuvimos
Anduvieron	Estuvieron	Tuvieron

Anduvimos a caballo en la granja – We rode horses in the farm.

Estuviste preso muchos años – You were in jail for many years.

Tuve una infancia muy traumática – I had a very difficult childhood.

No accent and the three verbs follow the same patter in the Preterit.

Caber – Fit in	Poder – Be able to
Cupe	Pude
Cupiste	Pudiste
Cupo	Pudo
Cupimos	Pudimos
Cupieron	Pudieron

No *cupe* en la caja – I did not fit in the box.

No *pudiste* decir la verdad – You could not tell the truth.

No accent and the two verbs follow the same pattern in the Preterit.

Poner – Put	Saber – Know
Puse	Supe

Pusiste	Supiste
Puso	Supo
Pusimos	Supimos
Pusieron	Supieron

*Ella **puso** el dinero en la mesa* – She put the money on the table.

***Supiste** la verdad a tiempo* – You knew the truth on time.

No accent and the two verbs follow the same patter in the Preterit.

Hacer – Make	Querer – Want	Venir – Come
Hice	Quise	Vine
Hiciste	Quisiste	Viniste
Hizo	Quiso	Vino
Hicimos	Quisimos	Vinimos
Hicieron	Quisieron	Vinieron

*Ella **hizo** la comida anoche* – She made the food last night.

***Quisimos** venir contigo* – We wanted to come with you.

***Vinieron** a desayunar esta mañana* – They came for breakfast this morning.

No accent and the three verbs follow the same patter in the Preterit.

Hacer In the 3rd person singular, changes "C" **to** "Z" to maintain pronunciation.

Conducir – Drive	Decir – Say / Tell
Conduje	Dije
Condujiste	Dijiste
Condujo	Dijo
Condujimos	Dijimos

Condujeron   Dijeron

Ella **condujo** *el coche hasta su casa* – She drove the car home.

Dije *la verdad siempre* – I always told the truth.

No accent and the two verbs follow the same patter in the Preterit.

The third person plural of the *"J"* group is **"eron"** and not **"ieron".** Pay special attention.

Spell change in the Preterit – Cambio de escritura en el pretérito

To preserve the consonant sounds in the infinitives, several verbs change the spelling in the stem, thus keeing regular Endings.

Verbs in *"Car"*, *"Gar"* and *"Zar"* to maintain the *"K / G / S"* sounds in the first person singular *"Yo",* the *"C / G / Z"* change to *"Qu / Gu / C"* respectively. All other persons and all endings are regular.

Buscar – Search / Find	Jugar – Play
Bus**qu**é	Ju**gu**é
Buscaste	Jugaste
Buscó	Jugó
Buscamos	Jugamos
Buscaron	Jugaron

Cruzar – Cross
Cru**c**é
Cruzaste
Cruzó
Cruzamos
Cruzaron

Ella **buscó** *el tesoro perdido* – She searched the lost treasure.

*Ellos **jugaron** Golf ayer* – They played golf yesterday.

*Él **cruzó** la calle en rojo* – He crossed the street on a red light.

Notice the accent and consonant change in the First person singular "**Yo**".

Verbs that follow the same pattern as "Buscar / Jugar / Cruzar".

Abrazar a un niño – Hug a child.

Acercar un poco la silla – Move the chair a Little bit closer.

Agregar algo importante al tema – Add something important to the topic.

Almorzar en familia – Have family lunch.

Apagar las luces antes de dormir – Turn off the lights before sleeping.

Atacar al agresor – Attack the aggressor.

Aterrorizar al pueblo – Terrify the people.

Cargar con la culpa de alguien – Carry with someone else's fault.

Castigar al culpable es un deber – Punish the guilty is a duty.

Colocar las manos sobre la cabeza – Place one's hands on the head.

Comenzar la conversación en español – Start the conversation in Spanish.

Conjugar el verbo amar – Conjugate the verb Amar.

Danzar de la alegría – Danse of joy.

Destrozar el corazón de una mujer – Destroy the heart of a woman.

Edificar un templo para Dios – Build a temple for God.

Educar a los niños a temprana edad – Educate children while Young.

Empacar las cosas para el viaje – Pack things for the trip.

Enjuagar las lágrimas de alguien – Cleanse someone's tears.

Entregar el paquete temprano – Deliver the package early.

Gozar de la juventud – Enjoy youth.

Lanzar la bola – Throw the ball.

Llegar a tiempo – Arrive on time.

Memorizar la combinación de la caja fuerte – Learn by heart safe-box combination.

Negar la verdad es malo – Deny the truth is bad.

Organizar una fiesta de aniversario – Organize an anniversary party.

Pagar la renta atrasada – Pay due rent.

Pecar a cada momento en nuestros pensamientos – Sin every momento in our thoughts.

Pegar bien fuerte a los chicos malos – Hit hard bad boys.

Rezar es repetir palabras, orar es hablar con Dios – Rezar is to repeat words Orar is to speak with God.

Roncar mientras duermes – Snore while you sleep.

Sacar la basura – Put out the trash.

Tocar la puerta – Knock on the door.

Tropezar y caerse – Stumble and fall.

Verbs in "*Caer / Eer / Oer / Oír / Uir*" change "*i" to "y*" in the third person singular and plural of these verbs.

Caer – Fall
Caí
Caíste
Cayó
Caímos
Cayeron

Leer – Read
Leí
Leíste
Leyó
Leímos
Leyeron

Corroer – Corrode / Eat away
Corroí
Corroíste
Corroyó
Corroímos
Corroyeron

Caíste en mis garras – You felt in my trap.

Ella leyó mi libro – She read my book.

Las polillas corroyeron la madera – Bugs ate away the wood.

Oír – Listen / Hear
Oí
Oíste
Oyó
Oímos
Oyeron

Concluir – Conclude
Concluí
Concluiste
Concluyó
Concluimos
Concluyeron

Oí tu conversación con papá – I heard your conversation with dad.

Ella concluyó todos sus pendientes – She concluded all her pendings.

Notice the accent in all the conjugations with the exception of last person plural.

Verbs that follow the same pattern as "Caer / Eer / Oer / Oír / Uir".

Atribuir el hallazgo a los científicos – Attribute the Discovery to the scientists

Constituir una sólida defensa – Constitute a solid defense.

Construir la iglesia de la comunidad – Build the church of the community.

Contribuir con el bien común – Contribute with the common wealth.

Creer en Dios es un don – Believing in God is a gift.

Decaer la belleza femenina – Fade feminine beauty.

Destituir del poder a los corruptos – Dismiss corrupts from power.

Destruir la esperanza de un niño – Destroy the hope of a child.

Diluir la bebida – Dilute the drink (water down).

Disminuir en proporción – Diminish in proportion.

Distribuir la mercancía a los supermercados – Distribute merchandises to supermarkets.

Entreoír la conversación de los demás – Half-hear the conversation of others.

Huir de la responsabilidad paternal – Run away from fatherhood responsability (Flee).

Incluir los ingredientes principales – Include main ingredients.

Influir en la decisión del consejo – Influence in the board's decision.

Intuir el peligro y la maldad – Sense danger and evil.

Obstruir la justica – Obstruct justice.

Poseer el fruto del Espíritu Santo – Possess the fruit of the Holy Spirit.

Proveer la verdad y la justicia – Promote truth and

justice.

Recaer *en el vicio de las drogas* – Fall back the bad habits of drugs.

Recluir *los prisioneros* – Imprison the prisoners (Shut away).

Releer *el libro de español* – Read again the Spanish book (Reread).

Sustituir *al profesor de idiomas* – Substitute the Language teacher.

Some **"Ir"** verbs in the present tense keep the **"E / O"** of the infinitive in their Preterit conjugations **"E – IE" "E- I" and "O-U",** with the exception of the **third person singular and plural** where they change "E-I" and "O-U" in the third person.

Sentir – Feel	Pedir – Ask	Dormir – Sleep
Sentí	Pedí	Dormí
Sentiste	Pediste	Dormiste
Sintió	Pidió	Durmió
Sentimos	Pedimos	Dormimos
Sintieron	Pidieron	Durmieron

Sentí *tu fragancia anoche* – I felt your scent (small-fragance) last night.

Ella me **pidió** *una toalla para secarse* – She asked me for a towel to dry herself.

Dormiste *como un bebé anoche* – You slept like a baby last night.

Please notice the change in accent and the vowel changes as well.

Do not forget Ask and Aswers form.

¿Qué sentiste por mi cuando me viste? – What did you feel when you saw me?

Sentí algo extraño en mi pecho – I felt something weird in my chest.

No sentí nada cuando te vi. Ya te dije que no estoy enamorado de ti. – I did not feel anything when I saw you. I told you already that I am not in love with you.

¿Qué oyeron ustedes detrás de la puerta? – What did you hear behind the door?

Oímos a papá cuando te dijo que no. – We heard dad when he told you no.

No, oímos absolutamente nada. – We did not heard a thing.

¿Cuándo leíste mi libro? – When did you read my book?

Leí tu libro desde que me lo regalaste. – I read your book as soon as you gave it to me.

Lo siento mucho, pero no leí tu libro – I am sorry, but I did not read your book.

¿Cómo supiste cuándo llegué? – How did you know when I got here?

Porque llamé a tu mama y ella me dijo – Because I called your mother and she told me.

En realidad, no supe que llegaste, fue una coincidencia – I did not really know when you got here; it was a coincidence.

A little bit more – Un poco más

Salón de Clases - Classroom

Alfombra	Carpet
Computadora	Computer
Crayón / crayola	Crayon
Cuaderno	Notebook

Escritorio	Desk
Escuela / Colegio	School
Estuche de lápices / Caja de colores	Pencil box
Hoja de papel	Piece of paper
Lápiz	Pencil
Lápiz a color	Pencil crayon
Libro	Book
Luz	Light
Marcador	Marker
Mesa	Table
Mochila	Backpack
Pegamento	Glue
Pizarrón / Pizarra	Whiteboard / Blackboard
Puerta	Door
Regla	Ruler
Reloj	Clock / Watch
Resaltador	Highlighter
Silla	Chair
Teléfono	Telephone
Tijeras	Scissors
Ventana	Window
Transporte -	**Transportation**
Ambulancia	Ambulance
Auto / coche / carro	Car
Autobús	Bus
Autobús escolar	School bus
Avión	Airplane
Barco	Ship
Bicicleta	Bicycle
Bote	Boat
Camión	Truck

Cohete	Rocket
Helicóptero	Helicopter
Motocicleta / moto	Motorcycle
Moto taxi	Moto Taxi
Taxi	Taxi
Tren	Train

Exercises - Ejercicios

1- Conjugate the verb in the past tense:

Yo ___(hablar)_____ con Pilar acerca de esto.

Nosotros __(comer) ____ langosta en el restaurante.

Usted __(dar)_____permiso para salir de clase.

Ellos__(ir)_____a ver Tarzan en el cine.

Él__(ser)_____módelo en su juventud.

2- Write down sentences for each pair of verbs:
Anduve, estuve

_____

Tuviste, pudiste_

_____

Cupo, puso_

_____

Supimos, hicimos

_____

Quisieron, vinieron

_____

3- Determine which personal pronoun goes with each of the following verbs:

Dije

_____

Condujo

_____

Buscamos

_____

Jugaron

_____

Cruzó

_____

Abrazaste

_____

4- Answer the following questions:
¿Le agregamos azúcar a la torta?

_____

¿Almorzaron ellos juntos?

¿Apagaste la luz antes de salir?

¿Atacó al agresor cuando salía?

¿Cargué con la culpa de todos?

5-   Create questions from the following sentences:
Me caí de un árbol muy alto.

El óxido corroyó mi nevera.

Oíste el timbre la segunda vez que sonó.

Concluímos que no valía la pena.

Elisa decayó con la enfermedad.

Marcos diluyó la solución en el laboratorio.

Reading Comprehension:

1- ¿Por qué se les llama habanos?

_____

2- ¿Quién impuso un monopolio real del tabaco?

_____

3- ¿Cuál de los cuatro elementos que le brindan su calidad al habano es el más importante?

_____

4- ¿Cómo es la caja en la que se empacan los tabacos?

_____

Knowledge Base
Republic of Cuba - República de Cuba
Motto: Patria o Muerte, Venceremos - Homeland or Death, we shall overcome
Capital and largest city - Havana
Demonym - Cuban
Government - Unitary Marxist–Leninist one-party state
President - Raúl Castro
Vice President - Miguel Díaz-Canel[
Population - 2015 census - 11,239,004
Currency - Peso (CUP) - Convertible peso (CUC)
Calling code - +53
From 1993 to 2004, the United States dollar was

used alongside the peso until the dollar was replaced by the convertible peso.

Bible Verse - Versículo Bíblico

Porque por gracia sois salvos por medio de la fe; y esto no de vosotros, pues es don de Dios; no por obras, para que nadie se gloríe. **Efesios 2:8-9**

Lesson 4

Camino de Alfombras – Carpet's road

La pasada Semana Santa *he decidido* viajar a El Salvador, más específicamente a Ahuachapán. Allí *he visto* muchas cosas interesantes y hermosas, pero nada como las alfombras que los salvadoreños crean sobre las calles de sus pueblos y ciudades para que el Viernes Santo pase sobre ellas lo que llaman el Santo Entierro.

He llegado el día viernes y *he visto* la conmoción de los artesanos que *han dedicado* parte de sus vidas al arte de estas alfombras. El viernes Santo han de concursar en busca de hacerse acreedores del premio que da la Casa de la Cultura del Departamento de Ahuachapán. En este concurso *han participado* por años barrios, colonias, grupos religiosos, instituciones y familias.

El guía turístico me *ha explicado* que para conseguir los resultados que se disfrutan cada Viernes Santo, *ha habido* muchos días de trabajo y dedicación por parte de los concursantes. En primer lugar *han preparado* los materiales que habrán de usar.

Estas alfombras *han sido* siempre elaboradas principalmente con aserrín y se *han usado* anilinas para colorearlas de vivos colores, una zaranda, manguera, cubeta, tablas de madera y unas formas que ayudan al artesano en su trabajo. Estas formas pueden ser círculos, estrella, óvalos, pentágonos, cuadrados y pare usted de contar.

Me dice mi guía que el proceso *ha comenzado* mínimo con una semana de anticipación ya que el proceso de tinte del aserrín *ha sido* realmente arduo. *Han debido* primero refinar el aserrín, luego *han pigmentado* el aserrín, lo cual *han hecho* agregando a una cubeta agua, la anilina y el aserrín y lo dejan allí por al menos cinco días. Esto lo *han hecho* con cada color de aserrín que han de usar. Después *han secado* el aserrín al sol.

Cuando el aserrín *ha quedado* listo, el artesano *ha plasmado* el diseño de su alfombra en un papel y *ha decidido* el tamaño que ha de tener su alfombra. Después que le *han asignado* el espacio de la calle que le *ha correspondido*, el artesano *ha hecho* un marco con las tablas de madera donde habrá de vaciar el aserrín.

Se ha de llenar el marco de madera con aserrín sin color, se moja con la manguera y allí se pasa el diseño del papel, luego se *ha agregado* a cada figura el color que determina el diseño, así poco a poco las figuras *han ido* tomando forma.

Para finalizar algunos artesanos *han decidido* ponerles piedras, papeles de colores y otros para adornar sus alfombras y hacerlas más llamativas aún.

Ha sido increíble para mí ver el resultado de estas obras. *Han llegado* personas de todos los confines de Ahuachapán y sus alrededores, algunos *han llegado* en carro, otros en moto, algunos en bicicleta y muchos a pie.

También somos unos cuantos los que *hemos venido* de muy lejos haciendo uso de autobuses y aviones. *Ha valido* la pena ver tan bello espectáculo, *han sido* muchos los días que *ha durado* el proceso, sin embargo en segundos son destruidas todas las alfombras cuando sobre ellas *han pasado* quienes acompañan al Santo Entierro en procesión hoy Viernes Santo por la noche.

Word List – Listado de palabras

Camino de Alfombras – Carpet's road.

La pasada Semana Santa – Past Holy week.

Más específicamente – More specificly.

Los salvadoreños – Salvadorian people.

Viernes Santo – Holy Friday.

Santo Entierro. – Holy burial.

La conmoción de los artesanos – Craftsmen commontion.

Parte de sus vidas - Part of their lives.

Han de concursar - They have to compete.

Hacerse acreedores del premio – To win the Price.

Casa de la Cultura – Culture house.

Barrios, colonias, grupos religiosos – Neighborhood, Colonies, religious groups.

Instituciones y familias – Institutions and families.

Y dedicación por parte de los concursantes – And dedication by the contestants.

Los materiales – The tolos (materials).

Con aserrín – With sawdust.

Anilinas para colorearlas de vivos colores – Aniline to color with live colors.

Manguera, cubeta – Hose, bucket

Unas formas – Shapes.

El proceso ha comenzado – The process has started.

Proceso de tinte del aserrín – The coloring process of sawdust.

Realmente arduo – Really hard.

Que han de usar – They have to use.

El diseño de su alfombra – the design of their carpet.

Vaciar el aserrín. – Pull out the sawdust.

Se moja con la manguera – It is wet with the hose.

Hacerlas más llamativas aún – Make them more appealing.

De todos los confines - From all over the world.

En procesión – Procession.

Grammar Explanations – Notas gramaticales

The auxiliary verb "Haber – Have". – El verbo auxiliar "Haber – Have".

The auxiliary verb "*Haber – Have*". We have seen its only form "*Hay*" in the meaning of existence "*There is – There Are*".

We are now going to see its real conjugation as an auxiliary verb. Many native Spanish do not know how to conjugate this verb, because it is only use to form other time. Once again, do not mistake this auxiliary verb with any other verb; it is only used for form other past times as will see on this lesson and more to come. Its first use is to form the perfect these.

Past Participle – Pasado Participio.

Haber		Have.
Yo	he	I have
Tú	has	You have
Usted	ha	You (polite) have
Él	ha	He has
Ella	ha	She has
Nosotros	hemos	We have
Ustedes	han	You (plural) have
Ellos (as)	han	They have

Past Participle – Pasado Participio.

Since we have learned the auxiliary verb that goes with the perfect time, we now need to learn how to make the past participle of the verbs.

It is a very easy and simple process, just drop the *"Ar"* and add *"ADO"* or drop the *"Er / Ir"* and add *"IDO"*.

Hablar – Speak	Habl*ado* – Spoken
Comer – Eat	Com*ido* – Eaten
Partir – Leave	Part*ido* - Left

As you can see, it is the same ending for "ER" and "IR" verbs, so, it is easy to learn how to form it. Let us see them in action now.

Uses of the participle – Usos del participio
Perfect Tense – Tiempo Perfecto.

This time is formed with the conjugation of *"Haber"* in present plus the past participle of the verb. The perfect time refers to actions that have been or will be completed.

Yo he hablado - I have spoken.

Tú has hablado – You have spoken.

Usted ha hablado – You (polite) have spoken.

Él ha hablado – He has spoken.

Ella ha hablado – She has spoken.

Nosotros hemos hablado – We have spoken.

Ustedes han hablado –You (plural) have spoken.

Ellos (as) han hablado – They have spoken.

He hablado contigo muchas veces, pero nunca entiendes – I have spoken with you many times, but you never understand.

Hemos hablado mucho de nuestras vidas hoy – We have spoken a lot about our lives today.

Creo que hemos comido demasiado pescado – I believe we have eaten too much fish.

He partido desde Paris a las 9:00 am y aun no llego a mi destino – I have left Paris at 9:00 am and I still don't reach my destination.

The participle as an adjective – El participio como adjetivo.

When you use the participle as an adjective, *it must agree in gender and number* with the noun they are modifying. As an adjective, the participle indicates the result of an action or a state of being, just as in English.

*Estoy **cansado** de trabajar* – I am tired of working.

*Ella está **enojada** conmigo* – She is upset with me.

*Los libros están **cerrados*** – The books are closed.

The participle by itself – El participio solo.

Did you know that you don't have to conjugate verbs to use the participle? When you use it alone, it makes an *exclamation, interject or refer to a state of being or situation.*

*¿**Enojado** yo? Eres tú quien está **enojada**.* – Me, mad? You are the one who's mad.

*¿**Sorprendida**? Soy yo, tu amor **encontrado**.* – Surprised? It is me, your found love.

Referring to a situation that happens frequently or repeatedly.

*Siempre **rodeado** de lindas chicas* – Always surrounded by pretty girls.

*Siempre **enfadada** conmigo* – Always mad at me.

The participle as a noun – El participio como nombre o sustantivo.

The past participle as a noun often corresponds to the *"Ed"* object nouns in English. When using it as a noun, it must agree with gender and number.

El herido - The injured one.

*¿Qué pasó con **el herido**, mejoró o empeoró?* – What happened with the injured one, did he get better or worst?

El afectado - The affected one.

*El **afectado** por la noticia fui yo* – The affected one by the news was me.

El acusado - The accused one.

*Los **acusados** quedaron libres de cargos* – The accused ones were free of charges.

El ahogado – The drowned one.

*Las **ahogadas** permanecen en la* morgue – The drowned ones remain at the morgue.

El pintado - The painted one.

*Quise pintar la casa y **el pintado** fui yo* – I wanted to paint the house and the painted one was me.

El amado – The loved one.

El amado ya no es amado, más bien odiado – The loved one is not longer loved, but hated instead.

Participle with "Tener"

When using the participle with the verb "Tener" it indicates the result of a repeated or extended action.

***Tengo guardado** dinero para la Universidad* – I have saved money for the university.

*Te **tengo dicho** que no acepto excusas* – I've said repeatedly that I do not accept excuses.

***Tenemos pensado** visitarte mañana* – We have thought repeatly on visiting you tomorrow.

Participle with "Llevar"

When using the participle with the verb "Llevar" it indicates the accumulation of a continuous action.

***Llevamos ahorrado** 5,00 pesos* – I have safed 5,000 Pesos.

*Marta **lleva gastado** 15,000 pesos y no es mediado de mes aun* – Marta has spent 15,000 Pesos and it is not even half of the month.

Participle with "Dejar"

When using the participle with "Dejar" it indicates that the action has been completed earlier as a precaution.

*Te **dejé hecha** la maleta* – I've left your luggage

ready.

*Te **dejamos hecho** el desayuno* – We have left breakfast ready.

Do not forget the Ask and Answers form.

¿Has hablado con el profesor últimamente? – Have you spoken with the teacher lately?

*Si, **he hablado** con el profesor* – Yes, I have spoke to the teacher.

*No, no **he hablado** con el profesor* – No, I have not spoken with the teacher.

¿Cuánto llevas gastado este mes? - How much have you spend this month so far?

***Llevo gastado** como 25,000 mil pesos* – I have spent so far about 25,000 thousand Pesos.

¿Cuántos libros tienes guardados? - How many books have you saved?

***Tengo guardado** 5 libros* – I have saved 5 books.

¿Qué ha pasado con el acusado? – What has happened with the accused one?

*No, sé que **ha pasado,** pero creo que lo encontraron culpable* – I don't now what has happened, but I think he was found guilty.

Regular verbs in the participle - Verbos regulares en el participio.

Here you have a small list of regular verbs in the participle to improve your learning skills.

Actuar – **actuado**	Act
Amar – **amado**	Love
Bailar – **bailado**	Dance
Cambiar – **cambiado**	Change
Comenzar – **comenzado**	Start / Begin

Contar – **contado**	Count / Tell
Dar – **Dado**	Give
Enviar – **enviado**	Send
Estar – **estado**	Be
Pagar – **pagado**	Pay
Agradecer – **agradecido**	Thank
Caer – **caído**	Fall
Entender – **entendido**	Understand
Leer – **leído**	Read
Oler – **olido**	Smell
Proteger – **protegido**	Protect
Querer – **querido**	Want
Ser – **sido**	Be
Tener – **tenido**	Have
Valer – **valido**	Be worth / Value
Conducir – **conducido**	Drive / Conduct
Construir – **construido**	Construct / Build
Dirigir – **dirigido**	Direct / Lead
Discernir – **discernido**	Discern
Distinguir – **distinguido**	Distinguish
Dormir – **dormido**	Sleep
Ir – **ido**	Go
Pedir – **pedido**	Ask
Salir – **salido**	Go out
Vivir – **vivido**	Live

Irregular verbs in the past participle – Verbos irregulares en el participio

As always, we have irregular verbs in the participle, lucky for you almost 90% of the verbs and maybe more are regular in the past participle.

| Hacer – **hecho** | Do / Make |

Poner – **puesto**	Put
Ver – **visto**	See / Watch
Decir – **dicho**	Say / Tell
Abrir – **abierto**	Open
Escribir –**escrito**	Write
Romper – **roto**	Break
Descubrir – **descubierto**	Discover
Cubrir – **cubierto**	Cover
Morir – **muerto**	Die
Volver – **vuelto**	Return / Come back

Verbs with two participles "Regular and Irregular" – Verbos con dos participios "Regular e Irregular".

This is a tricky one and at the same time a very easy one. As you will see, some verbs have both "regular and irregular" participle. They are used as an adjective or as a verb. It is not uncommon to use the adjective form in more informal speech instead of the verb form. The irregular participle is the one use as an adjective and the regular participle is the one use as a verb.

Infitinive - Irregular Participle - Regular - Participle

Bendecir bendito - bendecido - Bless

El bendito – the blessed one.

*Te **he bendecido*** – I have blessed you.

Confundir - confuso Confundido - Confuse

El confundido – The confused one

*Te **he confundido*** *con alguien más* – I have mistaken you with someone else.

*Esto es **confuso*** – This is confusing. *Confuso is more used when saying "confusing".*

Corromper - corrupto corrompido - Corrupt
El corrupto – the corrupted one.
Se ha corrompido el Sistema – The system has been corrupted.

Despertar despierto despertado - Wake up
El despierto – The awaken one.
He despertado temprano hoy – I have waken up early today.
Despierto is also used to refer to a very skillful person, or street wise.

Imprimir impreso – imprimido - Print
El impreso – the printed one.
He impreso los documentos (*He imprimido los documentos*) – I have printed the documents. *We seldom use "imprimido".*

Maldecir maldito maldecido - Curse
El maldito – the cursed done.
Te he maldecido por tus pecados – I have cursed you because of your sins.

Poseer – poseso - poseído - Possess
El poseído – the possessed one.
Te ha poseído el maligno – The evil one has possessed you.
We seldom use "poseso".

Presumir presunto presumido - Show off
El presumido – The show off one.
He presumido mucho de ti – I have shown off a lot about you.

Presunto is more used in legal terms like:

El presunto – the so called / the alleged one.

El presunto asesino – the so-called murderer / the alleged murderer.

El presunto heredero – the co-called heir / the alleged heir.

Proveer   provisto proveído   - Furnish / Supply

El provisto – the supplied one.

He provisto (proveído) toda la información necesaria – I have supplied all the necessary information. *Provisto is more common than proveído.*

Suspender - suspenso suspendido - Suspend

El suspendido – the suspended one.

Te han suspendido del trabajo – You have been suspended from work.

Suspenso is more used when referring to suspense.

Freír / frito / freído   -   Fry

El frito – the fried one.

He freído (frito) la carne – I have fried the meat. You can use both of them.

Haber de + infinitive – Haber de + infinitivo

Since we already learned the conjugation of "haber", we are ready to learn this small trick. In some Spanish speaking countries you will hear this combination "haber +de+infitivo" which means "to have to, to be necessary, to be supposed to" but with a weaker sense. Remember, you can use the verb haber in any tense to use this combination.

Yo he de hablar contigo – I have to speak with you.

Has de hablar conmigo – You have to speak with me.

Hemos de terminar el trabajo – we must finish the work.

It is very simple and you just need to practice it. You will also see this combinations in songs and literature.

A little bit more – Un poco más

Formas / Figuras	Shapes
Círculo	Circle
Corazón	Heart
Cuadrado	Square
Diamante	Diamond
Rombo	Rhombus
Estrella	Star
Medialuna	Crescent
Ovalo	Oval
Pentágono	Pentagon
Rectángulo	Rectangle
Triangulo	Triangle
Negocio	**Business**
Accionista	Shareholder
Activo	Asset
Administración, gerencia	Management
Ahorros	Savings
Arrendatario	Lessee, tenant
Bienes raíces	Real estate
Bolsa de valores	Stock market
Bono	Bond
Cabildero	Lobbyist

Cámara de comercio	Chamber of commerce
Capital	Equity
Carta de crédito	Letter of credit
Comercio	Trade
Comprador	Buyer
Cuenta por cobrar	Account receivable
Cuenta por pagar	Account payable
Desempleo	Unemployment
Deuda	Debt
Distribuidor	Distributor
Endosar	Endorse
Equipo	Team
Estado financiero	Financial statement
Ética laboral	Work ethic
Fabricante	Manufacturer
Fecha de entrega	Delivery date
Fecha de vencimiento	Due date
Gasto	Expense
Hipoteca	Mortgage
Huelga, paro	Strike
Inventario	Inventory
Junta directiva	Board of directors
Mano de obra	Labor force
Marca comercial	Trademark
Mayorista	Wholesaler
Mercadeo	Marketing
Mercado	Market
Papeleo	Paperwork
Reembolso	Reimbursement
Retirar	Withdraw
Sindicato	Union
Sociedad colectiva	Partnership

Tasa de interés	Rate of interest
Venta al menor	Retailer
Venta al por mayor	Wholesaling

Exercises - Ejercicios

1- Draw the following shapes:

Circulo	Cuadrado

Diamante	Estrella

Ovalo	Triángulo

2- Fill in with the word from the list: Inventario, ahorros, comercio, capital, fabricante, préstamo.

El _____ se ha agotado, y el dueño

de la tienda no tiene suficientes _____

_____ ni _____ para pagarle al

_____. Así que tiene que ir al banco a pedir un

_____.

3-   Write one sentence for each pair of noun and
verb. The verbs should be in the participle:
Yo, estudiar

_____
Él, conocer

_____
Ellos, comer

_____
Casa, ensuciar

_____
Perro, coger

_____
Niño, Jugar

_____

Mamá, freir

_____

Nosotros, proveer

_____

Reading Comprehension

1- ¿Qué materiales se necesitan para hacer estas alfombras?

_____

2- ¿Cuánto tiempo toma hacer una alfombra de estas?

_____

3- ¿Quién organiza el concurso?

_____

4- ¿Quiénes destruyen las alfombras?

_____

Knowledge Base
Republic of El Salvador - República de El Salvador
Motto: Dios, Unión, Libertad - God, Unity, Freedom.
Capital and largest city - San Salvador
Official language - Spanish
Demonym - Salvadoran
Government - Unitary presidential constitutional

republic

President - Salvador Sánchez Cerén

Population - 2015 estimate - 6,377,195

Currency - United States dollara (USD)

Calling code - +503

The United States dollar is the currency in use. Financial information can be expressed in U.S. dollars and in Salvadoran colón, but the colón is out of circulation.

Bible Verse - Versículo Bíblico

Y sabemos que a los que aman a Dios, todas las cosas les ayudan a bien, esto es, a los que conforme a su propósito son llamados. **Romanos 8:28**

Lesson 5

Buen Provecho! - Enjoy your meal.

¿Recuerdas cuándo comimos en Malabo? *Hablabas* hasta por los codos y *disfrutabas* de cada delicia que *traían* a la mesa. Fue una excelente idea ir a un restaurante de comida típica de Guinea Ecuatorial.

No puedo olvidar cuando *traían* de entrada esa sopa tan exquisita como lo es la "Pepsup" me *decías* que recodarías esa sopa por siempre y que la prepararías al llegar a casa, *pedías* la receta al chef y la cocinarías para mí una noche especial. Esta sopa sustanciosa estaba preparada a base de pescado y con montones de ají, algo de sal, agua y un buen aceite de oliva. *Creía* que *llorabas* por lo picante que era, pero no fue así, en cambio *reías* de felicidad ¿Cómo sería posible que tan pocos ingredientes lograran un sabor como ese?

Pero aún no te *sentías* llena y *querías* seguir comiendo sin parar. Cuando *traían* la gallina en salsa de cacahuates, *pensabas* que soñarías con ese plato tan especial. Llamarías al chef nuevamente para que te dijera cómo preparar ese plato también. El chef te *decía* que era muy fácil de hacer: freirías la gallina troceada y cebolla picada en cuadritos. Después añadirías cacahuates molidos y caldo preparado con los huesos de la gallina, lo *taparías*, y a las dos horas de cocción *estaría* listo para comer. También te *decía* que lo acompañaras con plátano y yuca como guarnición.

Creía que *estabas* llena después de tal banquete, me *equivocaba* ya que al llegar el mesero cuando aún *estábamos* comiendo *solicitabas* la carta de postres, no *lograbas* decidirte por uno solo y *decías* pedir dos postres típicos de la región: una ensalada de frutas tropicales y unos buñuelos de plátano. La ensalada *tenía* como base hojas de lechuga que *estaban* cubiertas por rodajas finas de tomate y en el tope se *encontraban* cuadritos de guayaba, coco y papaya, para terminar la *bañaban* en una salsa a base de vinagre y miel.

Los buñuelos de plátano, según te *enseñaban* *debías* prepararlos haciendo un puré de plátanos maduros, *formabas* bolitas del tamaño de un huevo de codorniz y las *freías* en mucho aceite hasta que flotaran. Luego las *retirabas* del fuego, *dejabas* que se enfriaran y las *pasabas* por azúcar.

Y lo que nunca *olvidabas* fue que *acompañábamos* esta gran comilona con una bebida muy especial "vino de palma", nos *mostraban* a ambos fotografías del proceso de preparación. Primero nos *señalaban* que el mismo se *obtenía* a partir de las palmas aceiteras, *hacían* una incisión en el cogollo más alto y *colocaban* un recipiente para recoger la savia. Luego la *dejaban* fermentar en un lugar donde no *había* mucho calor porque de lo contrario se *avinagraba* y se *conservaba* en calabazas en un lugar fresco hasta que llegase el momento de consumirlo. Y a ti con lo que te gustan las bebidas alcohólicas sin importar lo que sea: cerveza, ron, whisky, vermú, coñac, vodka, y pare usted de contar. Este vino de palma te *parecía* el mejor.

La rica comida de Malabo que es una insuperable mezcla de la cocina europea y la cocina africana fue irresistible para ti. Después de nuestra velada y de todo lo que *comíamos* y *bebíamos*, no me *quedaba* más que desearte: ¡Buen provecho!

Word List – Listado de palabras

¡Buen Provecho! – Enjoy your meal (Bon appetite).

Hablabas hasta por los codos - Speak non stopping.

De cada delicia – From each delight.

Restaurante de comida típica – Typical food restaurant.

Esa sopa tan exquisita – That so exquisit soup.

Pedías la receta al chef - You asked the recepe to the chef.

Una noche especial – A special night.

Esa sopa sustanciosa – That healthy soup.

En cambio reías de felicidad – On the contrary, you laughed of happiness.

Comiendo sin parar – Eating non stopping.

Gallina en salsa de cacahuates – Hen in peanut sauce.

Dos horas de cocción – Two hours cooking.

Gran comilona – Big eater.

Una bebida muy especial – A very special drink.

Vino de palma – Palm wine.

Fotografías del proceso de preparación. –

Photograph of the prepation process.

Palmas aceiteras – Oil palms.

Una incisión en el cogollo más alto – An incisión at the highest sprout.

La savia – The sap.

Sin importar lo que sea – No matter what.

Una insuperable mezcla – An unbeatble mix.

Fue irresistible para ti – It was irresistible for you.

Después de nuestra velada – After our evening party (Soirée).

Grammar Explanations – Notas gramaticales

The imperfect time – El tiempo imperfecto (Pretérito Imperfecto).

Whenever you refer to what used to happen or what happened regularly or periodically in the past, you have to use the imperfect time. Ideally indefinite past or continuous or repeated or took place over a period of time or started in the past but continues into the present. It can be better represented by the English "**Used to**"do or "was"doing.

Verbs ending in "Ar" – Verbos en "Ar".

Hablar – Speak / Talk

Yo	habl*aba*
Tú	habl*abas*
Usted	habl*aba*
Él	habl*aba*
Ella	habl*aba*
Nosotros	habl*ábamos*
Ustedes	habl*aban*

Ellos (as)   habl*aban*

Hablaba con mi esposa todos los días – I used to speak to my wife every day.

Trabajaba todos los domingos antes de casarme – She used to work every Sundays before getting married.

Hablábamos sobre la vida cada vez que nos reuníamos – We used to talk about life every time we met.

Remarks:

As you can see, the first person "Yo" and the third person singular "*Usted / Él / Ella*" have the same conjugation. The subject matter or context can indicate whom you are referring or you just have to use the personal pronouns for better understanding.

Yo hablaba con mi esposa todos los días – I used to speak to my wife every day.

Trabajaba todos los domingos antes de casarme – I used to work every Sundays before getting married.

Notice the accent in "*hablábamos*". Make sure to remember it all the time and estress the pronunciation where the accent is.

Verbs ending in "Er / Ir". – Verbos en "Er / Ir".

Comer – Eat		Vivir - Live
Yo	com*ía*	viv*ía*
Tú	com*ías*	viv*ías*
Usted	com*ía*	viv*ía*
Él	com*ía*	viv*ía*
Ella	com*ía*	viv*ía*
Nosotros	com*íamos*	viv*íamos*
Ustedes	com*ían*	viv*ían*

Ellos (as)   com*ían*   viv*ían*

Yo comía helado con mis compañeros de clase – I used to eat ice cream with my class mates.

Nosotros comíamos en el restaurante chino todos los domingos – We used to eat at the Chinese restaurant every Sunday.

Ellos vivían una vida miserable antes de conocer al Señor – They used to live a poor life before meeting the Lord.

Remarks:

Make sure to use the personal pronouns when using *"Yo"* and *"Usted / Él / Ella"* to avoid misunderstandings and confusion.

Notice that in *"Er / Ir"* groups, all the conjugations have accent on *"í"*.

Use of the imperfect tense– Uso del tiempo imperfecto.

Whenever you are describing mental and / or emotional states or desires in the past.

Ella se sentía feliz con sus hijos – She was happy with her children.

Queríamos cambiar de trabajo, pero no podíamos – We wanted to change Jobs, but we could not.

When speaking about time and dates in the past.

Su aniversario era el 20 de mayo – Her anniversary was on may the 20th.

Eran las 11:00 de la noche cuando llegaste – I was 11 pm when you got here.

When you are describing a scene or person in the past.

*La ciudad **era** hermosa* – The city was beautiful.

*Nosotros **teníamos** 19 años cuando tú naciste* – We were 19 years old when you were born.

*Tu mama **era** delgada y **tenía** el pelo negro* – Your mother was skinny and had black hair.

*Recuerdo muy bien que **hacía** un calor terrible ese día* – I remember very well, it was extremely hot that day.

When you referring to actions that set the stage for other actions. In this case, you will use the imperfect verb first and then interrupt it with a pretetite verb.

*Yo **estaba** comiendo cuando tú **llegaste*** – I was eating when you arrived.

*Ella **estaba** cantando cuando el fuego **comenzó*** – She was taking a shower when the fire started.

*Nosotros **estábamos** saliendo cuando los hermanos de la iglesia **llegaron*** – We were going out when the brothers of the church arrived.

When you are speaking about actions repeated habitually.

***Jugábamos** todas las noches* – We used played every night.

*Todos los fines de semana las chicas **iban** de compra* – Every weekends ladies would go shopping.

Do not forget the Ask and Answers form.

¿Qué jugaban todas las noches? – What did you use to play every nights?

***Jugábamos** Dominó todas las noches* – We used to play Dominó every nights.

¿Comías otra cosa con tus compañeros o era solo helado? – Did you use to eat something else with your classmates or was it just ice crem?

Si, algunas veces **comíamos** *caramelos* – Yes, sometimes we used to eat Candy.

No, siempre **comíamos** *helado* – No, we used to eat ice cream all the time.

¿Por qué vivías en las calles? – **Why did you use to live on the streets?**

Porque no **tenía** ni *familia* ni *trabajo* – Because I did not have family or a job either.

¿Por qué tu hermano hablaba tanto? – Why did your brother use to talk too much?

Porque él **era** *hiperactivo* – Because he was hyperactive.

Attention to "ni – ni" when you want to use a double negative statement, you use "ni… ni".

No quiero **ni** *comer* **ni** *beber* – I don't want to eat nor to drink.

Ella no trabajaba **ni** *los lunes* **ni** *los martes* – She did not use to work Mondays nor Tuesdays.

Irregular verbs in Imperfect – Verbos irregulares en el Imperfecto.

Remember, **ALL VERBS** *are regular in the imperfect time with the exception of three "Ser / Ver / Ir".*

You migh say "more irregular verbs"… but guess what. There are only three irregular verbs in this time. No stem changes, no spelling changes.

	Ser – Be	Ver – See / Watch	Ir – Go
Yo	era	veía	iba
Tú	eras	veías	ibas
Usted	era	veía	iba
Él	era	veía	iba

Ella	era	veía	iba
Nosotros	éramos	veíamos	íbamos
Ustedes	eran	veían	iban
Ellos (as)	eran	veían	iban

Cuando yo **era** *joven, siempre* **jugaba** *con carritos* – when I was Young, I used to pay with toy cars always.

Cuando **veía** *que mi papá se aproximaba* **salía** *corriendo* – When I used to see my father approaching, I used to run away.

Cuando **íbamos** *a la escuela,* **peleábamos** *mucho* – When we used to go to school, we used to fight a lot.

Remarks:
Notice the accent in "*éramos*", also the accents in all voices for "*ver*" and the only accent in "*íbamos*".

Some phrases used with the imperfect time – Algunas frases usadas en el tiempo imperfecto.

A veces - sometimes
Cada día - every day / each day
Cada año - every year / each year
De vez en cuando - once in a while
Frecuentemente - frequently
Generalmente – usually
Muchas veces - many times
Mucho - a lot / much / many
Por un rato - for a while
Siempre - always
Tantas veces - so many times
Todas las semanas - every week
Todos los días - everyday
Todo el tiempo - all the time

A Little bit more – Un poco más

Bebidas - Drinks

Chocolate caliente	Hot chocolate
Café	Coffee
Café con leche	Coffee with milk
Café negro	Black Coffee
Café descafeinado	Decaffeinated Coffee
Jugo de fruta	Fruit juice
Jugo de naranja	Orange juice
Jugo de manzana	Apple juice
Jugo de toronja	Grapefruit juice
Jugo de tomate	Tomato juice
Limonada	Lemonade
Leche fría	Cold Milk
Agua	Water
Té	Tea
Té con limón	Tea with lemon
Licuado	Smoothie
Gaseosa	Soft drink
Aperitivo	Aperitif
Cerveza	Beer
Coñac	Brandy
Ron	Rum
Vermú	Vermouth
Vino	Wine
Vodka	Vodka
Whisky	Whisky

Exercises - Ejercicios

1- Write sentences with the following beverages:

Café

_____

Limonada

_____

Jugo de tomáte

_____

Cerveza

_____

Leche fría

_____

2- How frequently do you do the following activities:

Comer

_____

Ir al cine

_____

Ir a la Iglesia

_____

Pagar las cuentas

_____

Vacacionar

_____

Cepillarte los dientes

_____

3- Describe the following mental and / or emotional states using the imperfect tense:

Ella (querer)

_____

Nosotros (sufrir)

_____

Yo (sentir)

_____

4- Describe a person in the past tense using the following characteristics: Pelo largo y negro, piel bronceada, rasgos armónicos, delgada y baja de estatura.

_____

_____

_____

_____

Reading Comprehension

1- ¿Qué comimos ese día?

_____

2- ¿Cómo se prepara la Pepsup?

_____

3- ¿La cocina de Guinea Ecuatorial es una mezcla de qué dos tipos de cocina?

_____

4- ¿Qué bebimos durante la cena?

_____

Knowledge Base
Republic of Equatorial Guinea - República de Guinea Ecuatorial
Motto: Unidad, Paz, Justicia - Unity, Peace, Justice
Capital - Malabob
Largest city - Bata
Official languages - Spanish
National language - French, Portuguese.
Recognized regional languages – Fang, Bube, Combe, Pidgin, English, Annobonese
Demonym - Equatorial Guinean - Equatoguinean
Government - Dominant-party presidential

republic

President - Teodoro Obiang Nguema Mbasogo

Population - 2015 estimate - 1,222,442

Currency - Central African CFA franc (XAF)

Calling code - +240

Bible Verse - Versículo Bíblico

Venid a mí todos los que estáis trabajados y cargados, que yo os haré descansar. Llevad mi yugo sobre vosotros, y aprended de mí, que soy manso y humilde de corazón; y hallaréis descanso para vuestras almas; porque mi yugo es fácil, y ligera mi carga. **Mateo 11:28-30**

Lesson 6

Huevos Rancheros – Ranchero's eggs

Estas vacaciones ***estaríamos volando*** hasta Acapulco, allí estaríamos por una semana. Llegamos al hotel muy tarde en la noche, sólo tuvimos tiempo de chequearnos, ir a nuestra habitación y dormir.

La mañana siguiente estaríamos despiertos bien temprano para así ***estar disfrutando*** de las hermosas playas a lo largo del día. Pero primero lo primero, mi esposa ha dicho: "***Estoy muriendo*** de hambre", así que corrimos al restaurante del hotel para desayunar antes de encaminarnos al mar.

Recuerdo que ***estábamos caminando*** hacia el restaurante cuando nos hemos encontrado con unos amigos mexicanos con quienes quedamos de acuerdo para pasear en su yate, nos acompañaron a desayunar. Estábamos sentados a la mesa y nos ***estarían trayendo*** el menú en un santiamén.

Parecía prometedor, ***estaban ofreciendo*** diversos manjares, muy internacionales todos ello. Había huevos con jamón, panquecas con queso y mermelada, tostadas con mantequilla y hasta yogur con miel. ***Estaba pensando*** qué pedir cuando uno de nuestros amigos, nos pidió que lo dejásemos en sus manos que quería que probásemos un rico desayuno mexicano, "huevos rancheros".

Con ingenuidad le pregunté a mi amigo, ¿no serán muy picantes verdad? Y él respondió con una sonrisa, claro que no, nada picantes. Le dije que estaba nervioso ya que le temía al picante. Él dijo que si se estaba en México y no se comía huevos rancheros al desayuno era como no haber venido. Así que estaría convencido y hemos aceptado comer lo que se nos ofrecía.

Cuando el mesero *estaba dirigiéndose* a nuestra mesa vimos con sorpresa unos llamativos platos con una base de tortilla, un pico de gallo sobre estas y encima lo que parecían unos inofensivos huevos fritos. Mi esposa y yo estábamos tan hambrientos que *estaríamos metiéndonos* el primer bocado de inmediato. Al unísono *estuvimos gritando* que necesitábamos agua y nuestros ojos se llenaron de lágrimas y se sonrojaron.

Nuestros amigos mexicanos *estaban riendo* sin parar y no paraban de repetir: "Pero si no son nada picantes". Allí *estábamos aprendiendo* nuestra primera lección de la gastronomía mexicana. Si un mexicano te dice que no pica nada, de seguro para ti será bastante picante, si dice que tan sólo pica un poco será realmente muy pero muy picante y si llegan a decirte que pica de verdad, será mejor que salgas corriendo porque son platos elaborados con tanto chile que *estarías* por horas *tratando* de aliviar el ardor de tu lengua y garganta.

La cocina mexicana es una delicia siempre y cuando se pida sin o con muy poquito chile, de otra manera *estarás sintiendo* como que tienes un incendio en la boca y que no lo puedes apagar. Para los mexicanos el chile es la base de sus salsas y condimentos, comienzan a comerlo desde niños y se acostumbran a este y cada vez piden más.

Son muchas las versiones que *estarían corriendo* de cómo los mexicanos comenzaron a hacer del picante una de sus tradiciones, pero yo estuve encantado con la que nos relató uno de nuestros amigos, ya que siempre he sido un romántico perdido. Nos contó que se hiso popular porque en muchos pueblos de México cuando un hombre iba a pedir la mano de una mujer a su casa, este *estaría siendo* puesto a prueba por parte de su familia política.

La familia de la novia *estaría* durante el día *preparando* un banquete para los novios y al llegar la noche la comida del novio sería muy especial, su plato estaría tan lleno de chiles que le sería casi imposible de resistir. Si el novio no botaba una lágrima durante o después de la comida se le consideraba digno y un excelente futuro esposo para la chica de la que *estaba pidiendo* la mano.

Cada vez que alguien me pregunta de nuestro viaje a México y especialmente de su gastronomía estaré diciendo que deberán estar muy pendientes, ya que su comida es siempre muy sabrosa pero también muy picosa.

Word List – Listado de palabras
Huevos Rancheros – Ranchero's Eggs.
Tiempo de chequearnos – Time to check us in.
La mañana siguiente - Next morning.
Hermosas playas – Beautiful beaches.
A lo largo del día – Throughout the day.

Pero primero lo primero – But first thing first.

Estoy muriendo de hambre – I am starving.

Antes de encaminarnos al mar – Before walking to the ocean.

Quedamos de acuerdo – We agreed.

Para pasear en su yate – To give a ride on their yacht.

En un santiamén – Right away.

Parecía prometedor – It looked promising.

Diversos manjares – Different delights.

Panquecas con queso – Pancakes with cheese.

Que lo dejásemos en sus manos – That we leave it on his hands.

Que probásemos – That we tried.

Con ingenuidad – Naively.

¿No serán muy picantes verdad? – They are not very spicy, aren't they?

Claro que no, nada picantes – Of course not, not spicy at all.

Le temía al picante – I was afraid of spicy.

Era como no haber venido – It was as if we have never come.

Unos llamativos platos – A very appealing dishes.

Con una base de tortilla – With a tortilla base.

Un pico de gallo – With a rooster beak.

Y encima lo que parecían – And on top of that, what they look like.

Unos inofensivos huevos fritos – Harmless fried eggs.

Tan hambrientos – So hungry.

El primer bocado de inmediato – The first bite inmediately.

Al unísono – All at once.

Nuestros ojos se llenaron de lágrimas – Our eyes were full with tears.

Nuestros ojos se sonrojaron – Our eyes were redened.

Estaban riendo sin parar – They were laughing non-stopping.

Pero si no son nada picantes – But they are not spicy at all.

Gastronomía mexicana – Mexican gastronomy.

Bastante picante – Spicy enough.

Aliviar el ardor – Relieve the burn.

Es una delicia – It is a delight.

Siempre y cuando – As long as.

Muy poquito chile – Very little chile.

Un incendio en la boca – A fire in the mouth.

Y que no lo puedes apagar – And that you cannot light off.

Salsas y condimentos – Sauces and condiments.

Un romántico perdido – A romantic (A lost romantic).

Pedir la mano – Ask the hand in marriage.

Estaría siendo puesto a prueba – It would be put to test.

Familia política – Political family.

Preparando un banquete – Preparing a package.

Los novios – The grooms (Bride and groom).

Tan lleno de chiles – So full of chile.

Casi imposible de resistir – Almost impossible to resist.

No botaba una lágrima – Not shedding a tear.

Durante o después de la comida – While or after

the food.

Se le consideraba digno - It is considered worthy.

Y un excelente futuro esposo – And an excellent future husband.

Estar muy pendientes – Be very aware.

Pero también muy picosa – But also very spicy.

Grammar Explanations – Notas gramaticales

Gerund in the main 5 tenses – El gerundio en los 5 tiempos principales.

We have seen so far the "*Present tense, the simple past, the future, the conditional, the perfect and imperfect tense*". Plus the gerund in the present tense only.

We will now learn how to use the gerund in all the times we have learned to so far. The structure is the same and the pattern as well. You just need to remember the conjugation of the verb "***Estar***" for each one of these different tenses.

Gerund in the present tense – El gerundio en el tiempo presente.

Yo	estoy	volando
Tú	estás	volando
Usted / Él / Ella	está	volando
Nosotros	estamos	volando
Ustedes / Ellos (as)	están	volando

*El piloto **está volando** el avión* – The pilot is flying the plane.

*Los pájaros **están volando** muy alto* – Birds are flying too high.

*El helicóptero **está volando** muy bajito* – The

helicopter is flying too low.

Gerund in the simple past or Preterit form – El gerundio en el pasado simple o pretérito.

Yo	estuve	fumando
Tú	estuviste	fumando
Usted / Él / Ella	estuvo	fumando
Nosotros	estuvimos	fumando
Ustedes / Ellos (as)	estuvieron	fumando

Ella **estuvo fumando** *por dos días* – She was smoking for two days.

Nosotros **estuvimos trabajando** *por una semana sin parar* – We were working for a week non-stopping.

Ustedes **estuvieron bebiendo** *toda la noche* – You were drinking all night long.

If you remember the correct use of the imperfect, you will not have any issues at all. Remember, the simple past or Preterit is for actions that ended.

Gerund in the future tense – El gerundio en el tiempo futuro.

Yo	estaré	abordando
Tú	estarás	abordando
Usted / Él / Ella	estará	abordando
Nosotros	estaremos	abordando
Ustedes / Ellos (as)	estarán	abordando

Usted **estará abordando** *el avión a las 5 de la tarde de hoy* – You will be boarding the plane at 5 in the afternoon today.

Estaremos reportando *desde la capital de Argentina los últimos acontecimientos* – We will be reporting from the capital of Argentina the latest events.

Estaré esperando *por ti a las 8 pm esta noche* – I

will be waiting for you at 8 pm tonight.

Gerund in the conditional tense – El gerundio en tiempo condicional.

Yo	estaría	cambiando
Tú	estarías	cambiando
Usted / Él / Ella	estaría	cambiando
Nosotros	estaríamos	cambiando
Ustedes / Ellos (as)	estarían	cambiando

Estaríamos cambiando el dinero ahora, pero lo perdimos – We would be cashing the money now, but we lost it.

Yo estaría besándote en estos momentos, pero me rompiste el corazón – I would be kissing you at this momento, but you broke my heart.

Ellos estarían viendo televisión, pero se les dañó – They would be watching TV, but it is broken.

Gerund in the imperfect tense – El gerundio en el tiempo imperfecto.

Yo	estaba	imaginando
Tú	estabas	imaginando
Usted / Él / Ella	estaba	imaginando
Nosotros	estábamos	imaginando
Ustedes / Ellos (as)	estaban	imaginando

Yo estaba imaginándome mi vida contigo – I was imagining my life with you.

Ella estaba cantando cuando llegó el pastor – She was singing when the pastor arrived.

Él estaba paseando cuando el carro lo chocó – He was going for a walk when the car hit him.

Ellas estaban tocando el piano al momento del terremoto – They were playing the piano at the moment of the earthquake.

Gerund in the perfect time – El gerundio en el tiempo perfecto.

Yo he   estado   suponiendo
Tú has   estado   suponiendo
Usted / Él / Ella ha   estado   suponiendo
Nosotros hemos   estado   suponiendo
Ustedes / Ellos (as) han estado suponiendo

He estado suponiendo que llegarías hoy, pero nunca me confirmaste. – I have been guessing that you would arrive today, but you never confirmed.

Ha estado lloviendo los últimos dos días – It has been raining these past two days.

Ha estado nevando mucho últimamente – It has been snowing a lot lately.

Ella ha estado necesitando una mano amiga, pero nunca estás presente – She has been needing a friendly hand, but you are never around.

As always, do not forget the Ask and Answers form.

¿Estás hablando conmigo? – are you talking to me?

Si, estoy hablando contigo. – Yes, I am talking to you.

No, no estoy hablando contigo. – No, I am not talking to you.

¿Estuviste fumando anoche? – were you smoking last night?

Si, estuve fumando anoche. – Yes, I was smoking last night.

No, no estuve fumando anoche. No, I was not smoking last night.

¿Estarás trabajando mañana? – Will you be

working tomorrow?

Sí, estaré trabajando mañana. – Yes, I will be working tomorrow.

No, no estaré trabajando mañana. – No, I will not be working tomorrow.

¿Estarían ustedes jugando béisbol ahora si tuvieran bate y pelota? – Would you be playing baseball now if you would have bat and ball?

Sí, estaríamos jugando béisbol ahora si tuviéramos bate y pelota – Yes, we would be playing baseball now if we would have bat and ball.

No, no estaríamos jugando béisbol ahora si tuviéramos bate y pelota – No, we would not been playing baseball now if we would have bat and ball.

¿Estabas imaginándote tu vida conmigo? – Were you imagining you life with me?

Sí, estaba imaginándome mi vida contigo. – Yes, I was imagining my life with you.

No, no estaba imaginándome mi vida contigo. – No, I was not imagining my life with you.

¿Has estado imaginando cosas? – Have you been imagining things?

Sí, he estado imaginando cosas. – Yes, I have been imagining things.

No, no he estado imaginando cosas. – No, I have not been imagining things.

Adverbs of quantity – Adverbios de cantidad.

You have seen them all around the lessons. Now, you have them all together with some remarks for a better learning experience.

Además   -   Additionally / Besides

Eres testarudo y además es imposible hablar contigo – You are stubborn and besides it it impossible to talk to you.

Además de Jazz ahora estudias piano – Additionally to Jazz, you study piano now.

Algo   -   Sightly / Somewhat

Don't confuse it when it is used as a pronoun meaning "something"

*Me siento **algo** emocionado hoy* – I feel somehow excited today.

*Te siento **algo** extraña. ¿Te pasa algo?* – I feel you slightly odd. Is there something wrong?

Apenas   -   Barely / Hardly

Apenas puedo comer – I can barely eat.

Apenas te soporto – I can hardly stand you.

Bastante   -   Enough / Quite a bit

*Eres **bastante** inteligente* – You are quite intelligent.

*Tengo **bastantes** problemas en mi vida, no necesito los tuyos* – I have enough problems in my life, I don't need yours.

*Todavía tengo **bastante** familia allá* - I still have quite a bit of family there.

Casi   -   Almost

Casi te rompo la cara – I almost break your face.

Casi me matas del susto – You almost frighten me

to death.

*Estoy **casi** seguro que ella está en algo raro* – I am almost sure that she is in something strange.

Demasiado - Too much

*Creo que soy **demasiado** sexy, siempre me lo dicen* – I think I am too sexy, they always tell me.

*Eres **demasiado** importante para mí* – You are too important for me.

Más - More

*Nadie te ama **más** que yo* – Nobody loves you more than me.

*Te quiero **más** que a nada en el mundo* – I love you more than anything in the world.

Medio - Half

*La batería esta **media** muerta* – The battery is half-dead.

*La puerta de la nevera esta **media** abierta* – The door of the refrigerator is half-open.

*Como que estoy **medio** muerto* – It looks like I am half-dead (tired).

Menos - Less

*Eres **menos** social que tu hermano* – You are less social than your brother.

*Estamos **menos** cansados que ayer* – We are less tired than yesterday.

Mucho - Many / Much / Very / A lot

*Tenemos **mucho** trabajo* – We have a lot of work.

*Hay **mucho** que hacer* – There is much to do.

Muy - **Very**

*Tú eres **muy** loca* – You are very crazy.

*Los muchachos están **muy** sucios* – The boys are very dirty.

Poco - **Few**

It can be used as an adjective or a noun. It normally means "*few*".

*Él trabaja **poco** pero gana mucho* – He study a little but he earns much.

*Tu hermana es una chica **poco** educada* – Your sister is a Little uneducated girl.

Sólo - **Only**

If there is no chance of confusing it with *solo* the adjective, no need for the accent.

Yo sólo quería hablarte – I only wanted to talk to you.

Ella sólo come arroz chino – She only eats Chinese rice.

Tan / Tanto - **So / As / So much**

Tanto when it is used as an adverb, it is shortened to "T*an*" when coming before an adjective, adverb or a phrase functioning as an adverb or adjective.

*¿Por qué hablas **tan** rápido el inglés?* – Why do you speak English so fast?

*Trabajaba **tanto** que me dolían las piernas* – I used to work so much that my legs used to hurt.

Other useful expressions – Otras expresiones útiles.

Un kilo de	a kilo of
Un litro de	a liter of
Un plato de	a plate of
Un trozo de	a piece of
Un vaso de	a glass of
Una botella de	a bottle of
Una cucharadita de	a teaspoon of
Una docena de	a dozen
Una libra de	a pound of
Una pizca de	a pinch of
Una taza de	a cup of

A little bit more – Un poco más

Desayunos / Postres y Más – Breakfast / Desserts and More

Huevos	Eggs
Huevos Duro	Hard Boiled Eggs
Huevos Tibios	Soft Boiled Eggs
Huevos Revueltos	Scrambled Eggs
Huevos Fritos	Fried Eggs
Tocino	Bacon
Jamón	Ham
Frijoles	Beans
Queso	Cheese
Pan	Bread
Pan tostado	Toast
Jalea / mermelada	Jam

Mantequilla	Butter
Miel	Honey
Yogur	Yogurt
Arroz con leche	Rice pudding
Buñuelos	Fritters
Flan	Custard
Galletas	Cookies
Helado	Ice cream
Pastel / Torta	Cake / Pie
Al horno / Horneado	Baked
Al carbón	Barbequed
Frito	Fried
A la parrilla / Asado	Grilled
En escabeche	Marinated
Hervido	Boiled
Crudo	Raw
Ahumado	Smoked
Estofado	Stewed
Poco hecho	Rare
Término medio	Medium
Bien hecho / Bien cocido	Well-done

Exercises - Ejercicios

1- Change the verb to its gerund in the present tense:

Yo __nadar__ todas las mañanas.

Luis ____preparar___ la cena para su novia.

Ellos __correr____ para llegar más de prisa.

Ustedes ___comprar__ un auto de lujo.

2- Write sentences using the gerund in the simple past form with the following verbs:

Cocinar

_____

Caminar

_____

Viajar

_____

Comenzar

_____

Terminar

_____

3- Write down a four lines paragraph explaining what you will be doing tomorrow, using the gerund in the future tense:

_____

_____

_____

_____

_____

4- Write down a four lines paragraph explaining what you would do if you won the lottery, using the verbs in gerund in the conditional tense:

_____

_____

_____

_____

5- Fill in the blanks using these verbs in gerund in the imperfect tense: imaginar, comprar, sacar.

Yo _____ cuánto iría a gastar cuando

_____ tantas cosas en la boutique de

la esquina. Yo _____ cuentas a ver si podría pagarlo.

6- Change the tense of the verbs using the gerund in the perfect time.
Tú _____creer_____ en su amor por mucho tiempo.

Camila _____beber_____ demasiado en los últimos tiempos.

Ellos _____bañar_____ en la piscina.

7- Determine how often you do the following activities, using adverbs of quantity.

Cepillar el cabello _____

Bailar salsa. _____

Comer cangrejo _____

8- Describe what you had for breakfast this morning:

_____

_____

_____

_____

Reading Comprehension

1- ¿Cuánto tiempo duraría nuestro viaje?

_____

2- ¿Con quiénes nos encontramos cuando íbamos al restaurante?

_____

3- ¿Qué pedimos para desayunar?

_____

Knowledge Base
United Mexican States - Estados Unidos Mexicanos
Capital and largest city - Mexico City
National language - Spanish
Demonym - Mexican
Government - Federal presidential constitutional republic
President - Enrique Peña Nieto
Population - 2015 estimate - 119,530,753
Currency - Peso (MXN)
Calling code - +52
Spanish is the de facto official language of the Mexican federal government.
Bible Verse - Versículo Bíblico
Jehová es mi luz y mi salvación; ¿de quién temeré? Jehová es la fortaleza de mi vida; ¿de quién he de atemorizarme? **Salmos 27:1**

Lesson 7

¡*Qué Blusa tan Hermosa!* - What a beautiful blouse.

Para mañana *habré visitado* un taller panameño donde se elaboran las increíbles molas. Al llegar me encontraré de entrada con los más hermosos colores, que van desde azules hasta rojos. Pienso que me impresionarán que muchos de ellos sean de tonos frutales, color naranja, mandarina, cereza, frambuesa, fresa, melón, durazno y muchos más.

Al llegar *habré visto* a un grupo de mujeres de la etnia indígena Kuna haciendo un trabajo minucioso. Una de ellas se me *habrá acercado* para explicarme cuál será el proceso a seguir para lograr una pieza tan hermosa como la que yo *habré adquirido*.

Habrá comenzado por explicarme que se trata de un arte tradicional de su etnia, que se elaboran tanto en Colombia como en Panamá y que se ha convertido en un arte popular del que se precia su pueblo.

Nos *habremos acercado* hasta la primera estación y comenzará su explicación. Aquí *habrán escogido* el diseño con el que trabajarán, algunos de los diseños *habrán sido* muy sencillos y basados en figuras geométricas, mientras que otras *habrán lucido* intrincados diseños inspirados en la naturaleza.

Es aquí donde se *habrán seleccionado* los colores que se *habrán utilizado* en la confección de la mola. Estos colores *habrán sido* sólo dos o podrán llegar a ser hasta siete.

Luego *habrán cosido* juntas cuantas capas de telas vaya a tener la mola que se *habrá elaborado*. Y después de esto comenzará el arduo trabajo del cortado. Usualmente se *habrá cortado* en la primera capa la parte más grande del diseño y luego de las capas más internas se *habrán entresacado* los detalles más pequeños.

Ahora se *habrá dado* el momento de coser alrededor de cada uno de los cortes que se *habrán elaborado*, estas costuras *habrán sido* hechas a mano con diminutas agujas que *habrán conseguido* como resultado una costura muy fina y casi imperceptible.

Después de que cada costura se terminé *habrá sido* supervisada la mola por la jefa del taller quien *habrá aceptado* que esta pasé al sector de confección o la *habrá rechazado* para que se le hagan las correcciones necesarias. Al llegar al taller de confección las modistas *habrán decidido* en qué pieza *habrán plasmado* la mola terminada, estas *habrán sido* desde un sencillo tapiz decorativo hasta en un elaboradísimo vestido de novia.

Al acercarme hasta la caja *habré pagado* por la blusa que compraré para mi hija, mi aprecio por esta joya *habrá sido* inconmensurable después de ver en persona la cantidad de trabajo y dedicación que toma la creación de cada pieza.

Word List – Listado de palabras

¡Qué Blusa tan Hermosa! – What a beautiful blouse.

Un taller – A workshop.

Las increíbles molas – The incredible moles (blouses).

De entrada – From starting.

De tonos frutales – Fruits tones (colors).

De la etnia indígena Kuna – From the Kuna Indian ethnic Group.

Un trabajo minucioso – A meticulous work.

Una pieza tan hermosa – Such a beautiful piece.

Un arte tradicional – A traditional art.

De su etnia – From her ethnic Group.

Tanto en Colombia como en Panamá – In Colombian as well as in Panama.

Un arte popular – A popular art.

Del que se precia su pueblo – From what her people are proud.

La primera estación – The first station.

Y comenzó su explicación – And she started her explanation.

Muy sencillos - Very simple.

Basados en figuras geométricas – Based on geometric shapes.

Intrincados diseños - Intrincated design (complicated design).

Inspirados en la naturaleza. – Inspired in nature.

La confección de la mola – The confection of mole (blouse).

Capas de telas – Every layer.

Las capas más internas – The most inner layers.

Los detalles más pequeños – The smallest details.

Hechas a mano – Hand made.

Con diminutas agujas – With tiny needles.

Una costura muy fina – A very thin seam.

Y casi imperceptible. – And almost imperceptible.

La jefa del taller – The boss of the workshop.

Las correcciones necesarias – The necessary corrections.

Las modistas – The dressmakers (couturier).

La mola terminada – The finish mole.

Un tapiz decorativo – A decoration tapestry.

Un vestido de novia – A bride's dress.

Mi aprecio por esta joya – My appreciation for the jewel.

Incommensurable – Fantastic.

✒️ Grammar Explanations – Notas gramaticales

We have been speaking throughtout the units about the importance of Spanish accents. Let us see the phonetic stress and ccent marks in Spanish.

Remember that Spanish words have only one phonetic stress. The stress is marked with a written accent *(′)*.

🔒 Acute words – Palabras Agudas

You will notice that *"Agudas"* words have the stress in the last syllable with a written accent on it only if the last letter ends in "**N**", "**S**", or vowel.

El Japonés es un idioma difícil – Japanese is a difficult language.

¿Cuándo hablarás español? – When Will you speak Spanish?

Interesante conversación – Interest conversation.
Me gustaría ver el menú – I'd like to see the menú.
Syllable separations
Ja-po-n*és*
Ha-bla-r*ás*
Con-ver-sa-ci*ón*
Me-n*ú*

Grave words – Palabras Graves
You Will notice that "*Graves*" words have the stress on the next to last syllable with an accent on it, if the last letter is any consonant, except "**N**" or "**S**".

Me siento débil hoy – I feel weak today.
No estás siendo útil – You are not being useful.
El lápiz es azul – The pencil is blue.
Syllable separations
Dé-bil
Ú-til
Lá-piz

Proparoxytone words – Palabras Esdrújulas
You will notice that "*Esdrújulas*" words have the tress two syllables before the last one and they need an accent on it regardless of the last letter.

Me gusta esta cámara – I like this camera.

Tengo un dolor en el estómago – I have a pain in the stomach.

La lámpara está apagada – The lamp is off.

El pronóstico del tiempo no es bueno para hoy – Weather forecast is not good for today.

Syllable separations

Cá-ma-ra

Es-tó-ma-go

Lám-pa-ra

Pro-nós-ti-co

Sobreesdrújulas words – Palabras Sobresdrújulas

You will notice that "*Sobresdrújulas*" words have the stress three syllables before the last "*fourth-last syllable*" and they need an accent on it regardless of the last letter.

No hay dinero para compras, entiéndelo, no podrás comprar nada. – There no money for shopping, understand it, you will not be able to purchase anything.

Difícilmente podrás hablar con ella. – you could hardly speak to her.

El frasco está cerrado, ábremelo por favor. – The bottle is closed, open it for me, please.

Está interesante tu cuento, cuéntamelo de nuevo. – Your story is interesting, tell it to me again.

Syllable separations

En-tién-de-lo

Di-fí-cil-men-te

Á-bre-me-lo

Cuen-ta-me-lo

Perfect Future - Futuro perfecto

Since we are experts already with the auxiliary "*Haber*" and its conjugation, in addition to mastering all different times we have learned, let us move on to our next set. The perfect future is form conjugating the auxiliaty "*Haber*" in its future tense plus the past participle of the next verb. It is equivalent to "*Will have*" in English.

Futuro Haber Pasado Participio Hablar.

Yo	habré	hablado
Tú	habrás	hablado
Usted	habrá	hablado
Él	habrá	hablado
Ella	habrá	hablado
Nosotros	habremos	hablado
Ustedes	habrán	hablado
Ellos (as)	habrán	hablado

Para cuando llegues mañana, yo habré hablado con ella. – By the time you get here tomorrow, I will have spoken with her.

Habremos terminado el libro antes del verano – We will have finished the book before summer.

Ella habrá terminado el español antes de salir de la universidad – She will have finished Spanish before getting out of the university.

Nosotros habremos lavado la ropa en la mañana – We will have washed the clothes in the morning.

Héctor habrá salido para la iglesia a las 7:00 pm – Hector will have gone out to church by 7 pm.

Remarks:

Remember, you will always need to use the personal pronoun when using "*Usted / Él / Ella*" and "*Ustedes / Ellos (as)*", because they might confused the listener.

When using the future perfect you are describing what a person "*will have*" been doing at some point in the future, something that has not happened yet but is expected to before another action. It can also indicate probability of what "*might have*" or "*probably have*" happened.

Notice that "*Haber*" is irregular in the perfect future tense.

Do not forget Ask and Answers form.

¿Habrá ella terminado el español antes de salir de la Universidad? – Will she have finished Spanish before getting out of the university?

Si, ella habrá terminado el español. – Yes, she will have finished Spanish.

No, ella no habrá terminado el español. – No, she will not have finished Spanish.

¿Habrás hablado con ella para cuando llegue mañana? – Will you have spoken to her by the time I arrive tomorrow?

Si, habré hablado con ella. – Yes, I will have spoken to her.

No, no habré hablado con ella. – No, I will not have spoken to her.

A Little bit more – Un poco más

Profesiones – Professions

Electricista	electrician
Abogado	lawyer
Actor / actriz	actor / actress
Albañil	mason
Arquitecto	architect
Autor	author
Banquero	banker
Barbero	barber

Teach Yourself Spanish Level Two

Bibliotecario	librarian
Bombero	firefighter
Camarero	waiter / server
Cantante	singer
Carnicero	butcher
Carpintero	carpenter
Cartero	postman
Científico	scientist
Cirujano	surgeon
Cliente	customer
Cocinero	cook
Comerciante	businessman
Contador	accountant
Criado	servant
Cura	priest
Dentista	dentist
Editor	Editor
Empleado	employee
Enfermero	nurse
Escritor	writer
Estudiante	student
Farmacéutico	pharmacist
Fotógrafo	photographer
Funcionario/ oficia	civil servant
Ingeniero	engineer
Jardinero	gardener
Joyero	jeweler
Juez	judge
Librero	bookseller
Maestro	teacher
Mecánico	mechanic
Mecanógrafo	typist

Médico / doctor	doctor
Modelo	model
Músico	musician
Obrero	worker
Óptico	optician
Panadero	baker
Peluquero	hair stylist
Periodista	journalist
Pescador	fisherman
Piloto	pilot
Pintor	painter
Policía	policeman
Plomero	plumber
Profesor	professor / teacher
Programador	computer programmer
Químico (chemist)	pharmacist
Relojero	watchmaker
Sastre	tailor
Secretaria	secretary
Soldado	soldier
Vendedor	salesman
Zapatero	shoemaker
Pescados y Mariscos –	**Fish and Seafood**
Almejas	Clams
Anchoas	Anchovies
Anguila	Eel
Arenque	Herring
Atún	Tuna
Bacalao	Cod
Calamares	Squid
Camarones	Shrimp

Cangrejo	Crab
Langosta	Lobster
Langostino	Crayfish
Mero	Bass
Ostras	Oysters
Pulpo	Octopus
Salmón	Salmon
Sardinas	Sardines
Trucha	Trout
Frutas	**Fruits**
Albaricoque	Apricot
Arándano	Blueberry
Banano	Banana
Caimito	Star Apple
Cereza	Cherry
Ciruela	Plum
Ciruela seca	Prune
Coco	Coconut
Durazno	Peach
Frambuesa	Raspberry
Granada	Pomegranate
Granadilla / Maracuyá	Passion Fruit
Guanábana	Soursop
Guayaba	Guava
Higos	Figs
Lima	Lime
Limón	Lemon
Mamey / Zapote	Mamey / Sapote
Mandarina	Mandarin
Mango	Mango
Manzana	Apple
Melón	Melon

Mora	Blackberry
Naranja	Orange
Níspero	Loquat
Papaya / Lechosa	Papaya
Pasas	Raisins
Pera	Pear
Piña / Ananá	Pineapple
Pitahaya	Dragon Fruit
Plátano	Plantain
Sandia	Watermelon
Tamarindo	Tamarind
Toronja	Grapefruit
Uva	Grape

Exercises - Ejercicios

1- Write three acute, three grave, three proparoxytone and three sobresdrújulas words.

2- Decide if the following words are acute, graves, paroxytone or sobresdrújulas:

Canción

Ajá

Cuéntamelo_____

Panamá _____

Antepenúltima _____

Teléfono _____

3- Write down the perfect future for the following verbs according to the person on each line.
Yo, cocinar

_____

Él, viajar

_____

Nosotros, vaciar

_____

Ellos, practicar

_____

Usted, reconocer

_____-_____

4- Determine what profession does each of the following sentences refer to?
Cura y Alivia las enfermedades.

_____

Repara goteos y problemas de tuberías

_____

Enseña en la escuela.

_____

Trabaja con madera y elabora muebles.

_____

Vuela aviones y helicópteros.

_____

Apresa a los delincuentes.

_____

Apaga incendios.

_____

Corta el cabello.

_____

5- Write down which are your three favorite fruits and your three least favorite ones.

Favorite_____

Least
favorite_____

6- Write a five lines recipe which main ingredients are fish and seafood.

Knowledge Base

Republic of Panama - República de Panamá

Motto: Pro Mundi Beneficio - For the Benefit of the World

Capital and largest city - Panama City

Official language - Spanish

Demonym - Panamanian

Government - Unitary presidential constitutional republic

President - Juan Carlos Varela

Vice President - Isabel Saint Malo

Population - 2015 estimate - 3,929,141

Currency - Balboa (PAB) - United States dollar (USD)

Calling code - +507

Bible Verse - Versículo Bíblico

El Señor no retarda su promesa, según algunos la tienen por tardanza, sino que es paciente para con nosotros, no queriendo que ninguno perezca, sino que todos procedan al arrepentimiento. **2 Pedro 3:9**

Conclusion

Thank you very much for selecting for your learning experience Teach Yourself Spanish By Yeral Ogando. Luckily, you've reached the end of this level, therefore, you are ready to speak Spanish with anyone. It is time to start LEVEL THREE.

I encourage you to continue practicing and speaking Spanish at all times, as I have already said Practice makes perfect. Visit my websites for more information.

Dios te bendiga y nos vemos la próxima vez.

Dr. Yeral Ogando
www.aprendeis.com

BONUS PAGE

Dear Reader,

You need to download the MP3 Audio files to follow this unique method gradually. Please visit our website at:

http://aprendeis.com/spanish-audio2/
The username is "spanish"
The password is "spanish122017"

Just download the Zip File and you are ready to start your learning experience.

If you want to share your experience, comments or possible question, you may always reach me at info@aprendeis.com

Remember:
Reviews can be tough to come by these days, and you, the reader, have the power to make or break a book. If you have the time, share your review or comments with me.

Thank you so much for reading Teach Yourself Spanish and for spending time with me.

In gratitude,
Dr. Yeral E. Ogando

Exercises' answers – Respuesta de los ejercicios

Lesson 1.
1   es el hermano de mi padre
el hijo de mi tío
la mama de mi abuela
el hijo de mi papa
la esposa de mi papa
el hermano de mi esposa
2   compraría muchas cosas
viajaría a Francia
no comería
no saldría a la calle
estaría muy feliz
3   más inteligente
más grande
tan inteligente
más sabio
tan grande
4   El peor
El mejor
El más grande
El más gordo
Celebérrimo

Lesson 2.
1   Con, Desde, Contra, Hasta, Para, Por, Según,

Sin, Tras.
2 Voy a la iglesia.
3 Vamos a dormir bien
4 Vamos a pie a la escuela
5 Te presento a Carlos
6 El desayuno es la 7
7 Nosotros estamos en la iglesia
8 El dinero está en mi cartera
9 Voy al cine en autobús
10 *El espectáculo es en vivo*
11 Salgo para la iglesia
12 Este regalo es para ella
13 El trabajo es para mañana
14 Estudio para aprender
15 Es un cepillo para cepillarse
16 Para la edad de nosotros, trabajamos demasiado
17 Para mi es demasiado amargo
18 ¿Para qué quieres el dinero?
Para comprar un carro.
No estoy para hablar
19 Caminamos por las calles de Paris
Te envío la invitación por email
Por ti lo hare
Me siento en la computadora por 12 horas
Trabajo por las noches
Me bebo la cerveza por ti
20 Por ahora estudiamos
Por cierto, tengo hambre.
Por fin, terminamos
21 Llego alrededor de las 5
Llego antes de las 4

22 A fines de febrero terminamos
A mediados de marzo iniciamos

23 Voy a comer pescado hoy
Voy a la iglesia el domingo

24 ¿A dónde vas?
Voy al cine.
¿Cuándo vas a trabajar?
Mañana en la mañana

25   hablaré, hablarás, hablará, hablaremos, hablarán diré, dirás, dirá, diremos, dirán

26   ¿Cuándo hablarás conmigo? Hablaré contigo esta noche.

27 ¿Cuándo terminarás el trabajo? Terminaré el trabajo en una hora.

28 Oiré, oirás, oirá, oiremos, oirán
Podré, podrás, podrá, podremos, podrán

29 Está nevando, Está lloviendo, Está nublado, Hay neblina, Hay una brisa, Hay viento, Hay mucho viento, Está húmedo, Hay sol, Tormenta.

Lesson 3

1   hablé, comimos, dio, fueron, fue

2   Yo anduve por Paris y estuve la ciudad.
Tú tuviste la oportunidad y no pudiste lograrlo.
El vaso no cupo en la caja y ella lo puso en la mesa.
Supimos la verdad e hicimos lo correcto.
Ellas quisieron comer mango y vinieron a casa.

3 Yo
Usted / él / ella
Nosotros
Ustedes / ellos / ellas

Usted / él / ella

Tú

4   Si, le agregamos azúcar a la torta.

No, ellos no almorzaron juntos.

Si, apagué la luz antes de salir.

No, no atacó al agresor cuando salía.

Si, cargué con la culpa de todos.

5   ¿de dónde te caíste?

¿Qué corroyó tu nevera?

¿Oíste el timbre la segunda vez que sonó?

¿Qué concluimos?

¿Qué pasó con Elisa?

¿Qué hizo Marcos en el laboratorio?

Lesson 4.

2   Inventario,   ahorros,   capital,   fabricante, préstamo.

3   Yo he estudiado inglés.

Él ha conocido a mi madre.

Ellos han comido arroz con carne.

Ellas han ensuciado la casa.

El perro ha cogido la comida.

El niño ha Jugado ajedrez.

Mamá ha freído el pescado.

Nosotros hemos provisto los recursos.

Lesson 5.

1   Me gustaba beber Café en la mañana.

Bebía Limonada cuando desayunaba.

No me gustaba el Jugo de tomate.

Me gustaba beber Cerveza

Quería Leche fría con el desayuno
2   Como todos los días.
Voy al cine una vez al mes.
Voy a la iglesia todos los domingos.
Pago mis cuentas siempre.
Vacaciono todo el tiempo.
Me cepillo los dientes todas las mañanas.
3   Ella quería hablar contigo
Nosotros sufrimos tu perdida.
Yo sentía mucho amor por ti.
4   Tiffany tenía pelo largo, una hermosa piel bronceada, era de rasgos armónicos, era delgada y baja de estatura.

Lesson 6.
1   estoy nadando.
está preparando.
Están corriendo.
Ustedes están comprando.
2   Yo estuve cocinando la cena.
Ella estuvo caminando mientras llovía.
Usted estuvo viajando por Europa.
Nosotros estuvimos comenzando la lección.
Ellas estuvieron terminando el trabajo.
3   Mañana estaré iniciando mi día muy temprano, porque estaré trabajando en un nuevo proyecto y estaré almorzando con mis colegas. Nosotros estaremos terminando el proyecto para final del día.
4   Yo estaría muy feliz si me gano la lotería y estaría comprando muchas cosas, estaría viajando a muchos países y estaría ayudando a mi familia.

Estaría construyendo una universidad y estaría llevando los hermanos de la iglesia.
5 Estaba imaginado… estaba comprando… estaba sacando…
6 has estado creyendo
Camila ha estado bebiendo.
Ellos han estado bañándose.
7 Me cepillar el cabello bastante.
Solo bailo salsa en las fiestas.
Casi no comer cangrejo.
8 Esta mañana desayuné huevos fritos, pan con mantequilla y café con leche.

Lesson 7.
1 Japonés, conversación, menú
Débil, útil, lápiz
Cámara, estómago, pronóstico
Difícilmente, ábremelo, cuéntamelo
2 grave
grave
esdrújula
grave
paraxytone
paraxytone
3 Yo habré cocinado
Él habrá viajado
Nosotros habremos vaciado
Ellos habrán practicado
Usted habrán reconocido
4 Enfermera
Plomero
Profesor

Dr. Yeral E. Ogando

albañil
piloto
policía
bombero
peluquero

5   Mis tres frutas favoritas son el mango, el guineo y lechosa.

Las tres menos favoritas son el zapote, el melón, la manzana.

, Hormiga.

Other books written by Yeral E. Ogando

Yeral E. Ogando comes from a very humble origin and continues to be a humble servant of our Lord Almighty; understanding that we are nothing but vessels and the Lord who called us, also sends us to do His work, not our work. Luke 17:10 "So likewise ye, when ye shall have done all those things which are commanded you, say, We are unprofitable servants: we have done that which was our duty to do."

Mr. Ogando was born in the Caribbean, Dominican Republic. He is the beloved father of two beautiful girls "Yeiris & Tiffany"

Jesus brought him to His feet at the age of 16-17. Since then, he has served as Co-pastor, pastor, Bible School teacher, youth counselor, and church planter. He is currently serving as the Secretary for the Dominican Reformed Church as well as the liaison for Haiti and USA.

Fluent in several languages Mr. Ogando is the Creator and owner of an Online Translation Ministry operating since 2007; with Native Christian translators in more than 25 countries.

(www.christian-translation.com),

The most exciting thing about his Translation Ministry is that thousands of people are receiving the Word of God in their native language on a daily basis and hundreds of ministries are able to reach the world through the work of Christian-Translation.com along with his translation network of 17 websites in different languages related to Christian Translation.

www.ingramcontent.com/pod-product-compliance
Lightning Source LLC
Chambersburg PA
CBHW071536040426
42452CB00008B/1040